50 St. Patrick's Day Lunch Recipes for Home

By: Kelly Johnson

Table of Contents

- Irish Potato Soup
- Corned Beef Sandwiches
- Shepherd's Pie Miniatures
- Colcannon Pancakes
- Green Spinach Quiche
- Traditional Irish Boxty
- Reuben Wraps
- Irish Bacon and Cabbage Sliders
- Guinness Beef Stew
- Smoked Salmon and Cream Cheese Bagels
- Irish Cheddar Stuffed Burgers
- Dublin Coddle
- Potato and Leek Frittata
- Herb-Crusted Irish Lamb Chops
- Green Veggie Wraps
- Irish Soda Bread Rolls
- Cheddar and Chive Biscuits
- Sausage and Mash Bites
- Spinach and Feta Stuffed Puff Pastry
- Lamb and Mint Meatballs
- Irish Carrot and Parsnip Soup
- Corned Beef and Swiss Cheese Panini
- Irish Cheddar and Apple Grilled Cheese
- Bangers and Mash
- Creamy Irish Mushroom Soup
- Colcannon Stuffed Mushrooms
- Spicy Irish Lamb Sausages
- Green Goddess Chicken Salad
- Cottage Pie
- Irish Style Tacos
- Smoked Salmon and Avocado Toast
- Irish Sausage Rolls
- Sweet Potato and Kale Soup
- Corned Beef Hash
- Green Bean Almondine
- Irish Egg Salad

- Salmon and Dill Quiche
- Savory Irish Pancakes
- Potato, Bacon, and Cheddar Muffins
- Irish Chicken Pot Pie
- Broccoli and Cheddar Stuffed Potatoes
- Irish Spiced Beef Sandwiches
- Spinach and Irish Cheddar Stuffed Chicken
- Green Pea and Mint Soup
- Irish Breakfast Burritos
- Warm Irish Lentil Salad
- Mushroom and Barley Soup
- Cabbage and Apple Slaw
- Irish Smoked Fish Chowder
- Green Pesto Pasta with Irish Cheddar

Irish Potato Soup

Ingredients:

- 4 large russet potatoes, peeled and diced
- 1 medium onion, chopped
- 2 cloves garlic, minced
- 4 cups chicken or vegetable broth
- 1 cup heavy cream
- 2 tablespoons butter
- 1 teaspoon dried thyme
- 1/2 teaspoon dried rosemary
- Salt and black pepper to taste
- 2 tablespoons chopped fresh parsley (optional, for garnish)
- 1 cup shredded Irish cheddar cheese (optional, for garnish)

Instructions:

1. **Prepare Vegetables**: In a large pot, melt the butter over medium heat. Add the chopped onion and cook until translucent, about 5 minutes. Add the minced garlic and cook for an additional 1-2 minutes.
2. **Cook Potatoes**: Add the diced potatoes to the pot and stir to combine with the onions and garlic. Sprinkle in the dried thyme and rosemary. Pour in the chicken or vegetable broth and bring the mixture to a boil. Reduce heat to low and simmer until the potatoes are tender, about 15-20 minutes.
3. **Blend Soup**: Using an immersion blender, blend the soup until smooth and creamy. Alternatively, carefully transfer the soup in batches to a blender and puree until smooth. Return the blended soup to the pot.
4. **Finish Soup**: Stir in the heavy cream and season with salt and black pepper to taste. Heat the soup over low heat until warmed through, but do not let it boil.
5. **Serve**: Ladle the soup into bowls and garnish with chopped fresh parsley and shredded Irish cheddar cheese if desired. Serve hot with crusty bread on the side. Enjoy!

Corned Beef Sandwiches

Ingredients:

- 1 pound thinly sliced corned beef
- 8 slices rye bread
- 4 tablespoons Dijon mustard
- 4 tablespoons mayonnaise
- 1 cup shredded Swiss cheese
- 1 cup sauerkraut, drained
- 4 tablespoons butter, softened
- 2 tablespoons chopped fresh dill (optional, for garnish)

Instructions:

1. **Prepare Bread**: Heat a skillet or griddle over medium heat. Spread a thin layer of butter on one side of each slice of rye bread.
2. **Assemble Sandwiches**: Place 4 slices of bread, buttered side down, on a clean surface. Spread Dijon mustard and mayonnaise evenly on the unbuttered sides of these slices. Layer each with shredded Swiss cheese, a generous amount of corned beef, and sauerkraut. Top with the remaining bread slices, buttered side up.
3. **Grill Sandwiches**: Place the assembled sandwiches in the hot skillet or griddle. Cook until the bread is golden brown and the cheese is melted, about 3-4 minutes per side. Press down lightly with a spatula to ensure even grilling.
4. **Serve**: Remove the sandwiches from the skillet and cut them in half diagonally. Garnish with chopped fresh dill if desired. Serve warm with pickles and a side of coleslaw or potato salad.

Enjoy your delicious corned beef sandwiches with a hearty flavor that's perfect for any St. Patrick's Day meal!

Shepherd's Pie Miniatures

Ingredients:

- **For the Filling:**
    - 1 pound ground beef or lamb
    - 1 medium onion, diced
    - 2 cloves garlic, minced
    - 1 cup frozen peas and carrots mix
    - 1 cup beef or vegetable broth
    - 2 tablespoons tomato paste
    - 1 tablespoon Worcestershire sauce
    - 1 teaspoon dried thyme
    - 1 teaspoon dried rosemary
    - Salt and black pepper to taste
    - 2 tablespoons all-purpose flour (optional, for thickening)
- **For the Mashed Potatoes:**
    - 2 cups mashed potatoes (prepared in advance or from a mix)
    - 1/4 cup milk
    - 2 tablespoons butter
    - 1/2 cup shredded cheddar cheese (optional, for extra flavor)

Instructions:

1. **Prepare the Filling**: In a large skillet, cook the ground beef or lamb over medium heat until browned. Drain any excess fat. Add the diced onion and cook until softened, about 5 minutes. Stir in the minced garlic and cook for an additional minute.
2. **Add Vegetables and Seasonings**: Stir in the frozen peas and carrots, tomato paste, Worcestershire sauce, dried thyme, and dried rosemary. Pour in the beef or vegetable broth and bring to a simmer. Cook until the mixture has thickened slightly, about 5-7 minutes. If needed, stir in the flour to thicken the filling further. Season with salt and black pepper to taste.
3. **Preheat Oven**: Preheat your oven to 375°F (190°C). Grease a mini muffin tin or small ramekins.
4. **Assemble Miniatures**: Spoon a small amount of the meat filling into each muffin cup or ramekin. Top with a dollop of mashed potatoes, smoothing them out with a spoon. If desired, sprinkle shredded cheddar cheese on top of the mashed potatoes.
5. **Bake**: Place the miniatures in the preheated oven and bake for 15-20 minutes, or until the mashed potatoes are golden brown and the filling is bubbly.
6. **Cool and Serve**: Allow the miniatures to cool slightly before serving. They can be enjoyed warm or at room temperature. Garnish with fresh herbs if desired.

These Shepherd's Pie Miniatures are perfect for parties or a fun twist on a classic dish, providing individual servings of this comforting favorite!

Colcannon Pancakes

Ingredients:

- **For the Colcannon:**
    - 2 cups mashed potatoes (preferably from about 4 medium potatoes)
    - 1 cup finely shredded cabbage
    - 1/2 cup chopped green onions
    - 2 tablespoons butter
    - Salt and black pepper to taste
- **For the Pancakes:**
    - 1 cup all-purpose flour
    - 1 tablespoon baking powder
    - 1/2 teaspoon salt
    - 1 cup milk
    - 1 large egg
    - 2 tablespoons vegetable oil
    - 1 cup prepared colcannon (from above)

Instructions:

1. **Prepare Colcannon**: In a large skillet, melt the butter over medium heat. Add the shredded cabbage and cook until softened, about 5 minutes. Stir in the chopped green onions and cook for an additional 2 minutes. Remove from heat and mix with the mashed potatoes. Season with salt and black pepper to taste. Let the colcannon mixture cool slightly.
2. **Make Pancake Batter**: In a medium bowl, whisk together the flour, baking powder, and salt. In another bowl, combine the milk, egg, and vegetable oil. Gradually add the wet ingredients to the dry ingredients, mixing until just combined. Gently fold in the prepared colcannon until evenly distributed.
3. **Cook Pancakes**: Heat a nonstick skillet or griddle over medium heat and lightly grease with a bit of vegetable oil or butter. Pour 1/4 cup of the pancake batter onto the skillet for each pancake. Cook until bubbles form on the surface and the edges look set, about 2-3 minutes. Flip and cook the other side until golden brown, about 2 more minutes.
4. **Serve**: Keep the pancakes warm in a low oven or covered with a clean towel while you cook the remaining pancakes. Serve the colcannon pancakes warm with a dollop of sour cream, a sprinkle of chopped green onions, or a drizzle of gravy if desired.

These Colcannon Pancakes offer a creative twist on a classic Irish dish, blending the comforting flavors of colcannon into a fun and savory breakfast or brunch option. Enjoy!

Green Spinach Quiche

Ingredients:

- **For the Crust:**
    - 1 1/2 cups all-purpose flour
    - 1/2 teaspoon salt
    - 1/2 cup cold unsalted butter, cubed
    - 1/4 cup ice water (more if needed)
- **For the Filling:**
    - 2 tablespoons olive oil
    - 1 medium onion, diced
    - 2 cloves garlic, minced
    - 4 cups fresh spinach, chopped
    - 4 large eggs
    - 1 cup heavy cream
    - 1 cup milk
    - 1 cup shredded Swiss cheese (or other cheese of choice)
    - 1/2 teaspoon dried thyme
    - 1/4 teaspoon nutmeg
    - Salt and black pepper to taste

Instructions:

1. **Prepare the Crust**: In a large bowl, whisk together the flour and salt. Cut in the cold butter using a pastry cutter or your fingers until the mixture resembles coarse crumbs. Gradually add ice water, a tablespoon at a time, until the dough comes together. Form the dough into a disk, wrap in plastic wrap, and refrigerate for at least 30 minutes.
2. **Preheat Oven**: Preheat your oven to 375°F (190°C).
3. **Cook Spinach**: In a large skillet, heat the olive oil over medium heat. Add the diced onion and cook until softened, about 5 minutes. Stir in the minced garlic and cook for an additional minute. Add the chopped spinach and cook until wilted and any excess moisture has evaporated, about 3-4 minutes. Remove from heat and let cool slightly.
4. **Roll Out the Dough**: On a lightly floured surface, roll out the chilled dough to fit a 9-inch pie dish or quiche pan. Transfer the dough to the pan and trim the edges. Prick the bottom with a fork.
5. **Pre-bake the Crust**: Place the crust in the preheated oven and bake for 10 minutes. Remove from the oven and let cool slightly.
6. **Prepare the Filling**: In a large bowl, whisk together the eggs, heavy cream, milk, dried thyme, nutmeg, salt, and black pepper. Stir in the shredded cheese and the cooked spinach mixture.
7. **Assemble and Bake**: Pour the filling into the pre-baked crust. Smooth the top with a spatula. Return to the oven and bake for 35-40 minutes, or until the quiche is set and the top is golden brown.

8. **Cool and Serve**: Allow the quiche to cool for at least 10 minutes before slicing. Serve warm or at room temperature.

This Green Spinach Quiche is a vibrant and flavorful option that's perfect for brunch or a light lunch, combining the richness of a classic quiche with the fresh, nutritious goodness of spinach. Enjoy!

Traditional Irish Boxty

Ingredients:

- 1 pound (about 4 medium) russet potatoes
- 1 cup all-purpose flour
- 1 teaspoon baking powder
- 1 teaspoon salt
- 1/2 teaspoon black pepper
- 1/2 cup milk
- 1 large egg
- 2 tablespoons butter or oil for frying
- 1/4 cup chopped fresh chives (optional, for garnish)

Instructions:

1. **Prepare Potatoes**: Peel and grate the potatoes using a box grater or food processor. Place the grated potatoes in a clean kitchen towel and squeeze out as much moisture as possible. You want the potatoes to be as dry as possible to get a crispy texture.
2. **Mix Dry Ingredients**: In a large bowl, combine the flour, baking powder, salt, and black pepper.
3. **Prepare Batter**: In another bowl, whisk together the milk and egg. Add the squeezed grated potatoes to the wet ingredients and mix until well combined.
4. **Combine Ingredients**: Add the potato mixture to the dry ingredients and stir until just combined. The batter should be thick and somewhat lumpy.
5. **Heat the Pan**: Heat a large skillet or griddle over medium heat and add a bit of butter or oil.
6. **Cook Boxty**: Spoon dollops of batter into the hot skillet, spreading them into about 1/2-inch thick pancakes. Cook until golden brown and crispy on the bottom, about 4-5 minutes. Flip and cook the other side for an additional 3-4 minutes. Repeat with the remaining batter, adding more butter or oil to the skillet as needed.
7. **Serve**: Transfer the cooked boxty to a paper towel-lined plate to drain excess oil. Garnish with chopped fresh chives if desired. Serve warm with sour cream, applesauce, or as a side dish with your favorite main course.

Traditional Irish Boxty are savory potato pancakes with a crispy exterior and tender interior, perfect for breakfast, brunch, or as a comforting side dish. Enjoy the authentic taste of Ireland with this simple yet delicious recipe!

Reuben Wraps

Ingredients:

- 4 large flour tortillas
- 1/2 pound deli corned beef, thinly sliced
- 1 cup sauerkraut, drained
- 1 cup shredded Swiss cheese
- 1/2 cup Thousand Island dressing
- 2 tablespoons Dijon mustard
- 2 tablespoons butter, softened

Instructions:

1. **Prepare the Tortillas**: Spread a thin layer of butter on one side of each tortilla. This will help them crisp up nicely when cooked.
2. **Mix Sauces**: In a small bowl, mix the Thousand Island dressing with the Dijon mustard. Adjust the ratio to taste, if desired.
3. **Assemble the Wraps**: Place each tortilla, buttered side down, on a clean surface. Spread a tablespoon of the Thousand Island-Dijon mixture evenly over the surface of each tortilla.
4. **Layer Ingredients**: On top of the sauce mixture, layer the corned beef evenly over each tortilla. Sprinkle with shredded Swiss cheese and distribute the sauerkraut evenly.
5. **Roll Up**: Carefully roll up each tortilla tightly, securing the fillings inside.
6. **Cook the Wraps**: Heat a large skillet or griddle over medium heat. Place the wraps seam side down in the skillet. Cook for about 2-3 minutes on each side, or until the tortilla is golden brown and crispy and the cheese is melted inside. Press down lightly with a spatula to ensure even grilling.
7. **Serve**: Remove the wraps from the skillet and let them cool for a minute before slicing. Cut each wrap in half diagonally. Serve warm with extra Thousand Island dressing for dipping.

Reuben Wraps offer a convenient, portable twist on the classic Reuben sandwich, combining all the familiar flavors in a crispy, delicious package. Enjoy this easy-to-make treat for lunch, a snack, or as part of a festive spread!

Irish Bacon and Cabbage Sliders

Ingredients:

- **For the Bacon and Cabbage Filling:**
    - 8 slices Irish bacon or thick-cut bacon
    - 1 small head of cabbage, finely shredded
    - 1 large onion, thinly sliced
    - 2 tablespoons vegetable oil
    - 2 tablespoons apple cider vinegar
    - 1 tablespoon brown sugar
    - 1/2 teaspoon caraway seeds (optional)
    - Salt and black pepper to taste
- **For the Sliders:**
    - 12 small slider rolls or mini brioche buns
    - 1/2 cup whole-grain mustard
    - 1/2 cup mayonnaise
    - 1 tablespoon chopped fresh parsley (optional, for garnish)

Instructions:

1. **Cook the Bacon**: In a large skillet, cook the bacon over medium heat until crispy. Remove from the skillet and drain on paper towels. Once cooled, crumble the bacon into bite-sized pieces.
2. **Prepare the Cabbage Mixture**: In the same skillet, remove excess bacon fat, leaving about 1-2 tablespoons. Add the vegetable oil and heat over medium heat. Add the sliced onion and cook until softened and slightly caramelized, about 8 minutes. Stir in the shredded cabbage and cook until tender, about 5-7 minutes. Add the apple cider vinegar, brown sugar, caraway seeds (if using), salt, and black pepper. Cook for an additional 2-3 minutes, until well combined and slightly caramelized.
3. **Combine Ingredients**: Stir the crumbled bacon into the cabbage mixture. Adjust seasoning with more salt and pepper if needed.
4. **Prepare the Sliders**: Slice the slider rolls or mini brioche buns in half. Spread a thin layer of whole-grain mustard on the bottom halves and mayonnaise on the top halves.
5. **Assemble the Sliders**: Spoon a generous amount of the bacon and cabbage mixture onto the bottom halves of the rolls. Top with the other half of the roll to complete the sliders.
6. **Serve**: Arrange the sliders on a serving platter. Garnish with chopped fresh parsley if desired. Serve warm or at room temperature.

These Irish Bacon and Cabbage Sliders are a flavorful and satisfying twist on traditional Irish fare, combining savory bacon with sweet and tangy cabbage in a convenient, handheld format. Perfect for parties, gatherings, or a special meal!

Guinness Beef Stew

Ingredients:

- 2 pounds beef chuck, cut into 1-inch cubes
- 2 tablespoons vegetable oil
- 1 large onion, chopped
- 3 cloves garlic, minced
- 3 tablespoons all-purpose flour
- 2 cups beef broth
- 1 cup Guinness beer (or another stout)
- 1 tablespoon tomato paste
- 1 teaspoon dried thyme
- 1 teaspoon dried rosemary
- 2 bay leaves
- 4 large carrots, peeled and sliced
- 3 large potatoes, peeled and cut into chunks
- 1 cup frozen peas
- Salt and black pepper to taste
- 2 tablespoons chopped fresh parsley (optional, for garnish)

Instructions:

1. **Brown the Beef**: In a large pot or Dutch oven, heat the vegetable oil over medium-high heat. Add the beef cubes in batches, being careful not to overcrowd the pot. Brown the beef on all sides, about 5-7 minutes per batch. Transfer the browned beef to a plate and set aside.
2. **Sauté Vegetables**: In the same pot, add the chopped onion and cook until softened, about 5 minutes. Stir in the minced garlic and cook for an additional minute.
3. **Build the Stew Base**: Sprinkle the flour over the onions and garlic, stirring to combine. Cook for 2 minutes, allowing the flour to lightly brown.
4. **Deglaze and Simmer**: Gradually pour in the beef broth and Guinness beer, stirring constantly to avoid lumps. Add the tomato paste, dried thyme, dried rosemary, and bay leaves. Stir well to combine.
5. **Add Beef and Vegetables**: Return the browned beef to the pot, along with any juices that have accumulated on the plate. Add the carrots and potatoes. Stir to combine.
6. **Cook the Stew**: Bring the mixture to a boil. Reduce the heat to low, cover, and let simmer for about 1.5 to 2 hours, or until the beef is tender and the vegetables are cooked through. Stir occasionally.
7. **Finish the Stew**: About 10 minutes before serving, stir in the frozen peas. Season with salt and black pepper to taste.
8. **Serve**: Remove the bay leaves before serving. Garnish with chopped fresh parsley if desired. Serve hot with crusty bread for dipping or over a bed of creamy mashed potatoes.

This hearty Guinness Beef Stew is rich and flavorful, with the deep notes of stout complementing the tender beef and vegetables perfectly. It's ideal for a comforting meal, especially during cooler months or festive occasions. Enjoy!

Smoked Salmon and Cream Cheese Bagels

Ingredients:

- 4 plain or everything bagels
- 8 ounces cream cheese, softened
- 4 ounces smoked salmon, thinly sliced
- 1 small red onion, thinly sliced
- 1 large cucumber, thinly sliced
- 2 tablespoons capers
- 2 tablespoons fresh dill, chopped
- 1 tablespoon lemon juice
- Salt and black pepper to taste

Instructions:

1. **Prepare the Bagels**: Slice the bagels in half and toast them to your desired crispness.
2. **Prepare the Cream Cheese Spread**: In a small bowl, mix the softened cream cheese with lemon juice, fresh dill, salt, and black pepper. Adjust seasoning to taste.
3. **Assemble the Bagels**: Spread a generous layer of the cream cheese mixture on each toasted bagel half.
4. **Add Toppings**: Top the cream cheese with slices of smoked salmon. Arrange the thinly sliced red onion and cucumber over the salmon. Sprinkle with capers and a bit more fresh dill if desired.
5. **Serve**: Arrange the assembled bagels on a platter. Serve immediately, or cover and refrigerate for up to an hour before serving.

These Smoked Salmon and Cream Cheese Bagels are a classic and elegant choice for breakfast, brunch, or a light lunch, offering a perfect balance of creamy, smoky, and fresh flavors. Enjoy!

Get smarter responses, upload files and images, and more.

Irish Cheddar Stuffed Burgers

Ingredients:

- **For the Burgers:**
    - 1 pound ground beef (80% lean)
    - 4 ounces Irish cheddar cheese, cut into small cubes
    - 1 tablespoon Worcestershire sauce
    - 1 teaspoon garlic powder
    - 1 teaspoon onion powder
    - 1/2 teaspoon smoked paprika
    - Salt and black pepper to taste
- **For Assembly:**
    - 4 hamburger buns
    - Lettuce leaves
    - Tomato slices
    - Pickles
    - Ketchup and mustard (optional)

Instructions:

1. **Prepare the Beef Mixture**: In a large bowl, gently mix the ground beef with Worcestershire sauce, garlic powder, onion powder, smoked paprika, salt, and black pepper. Be careful not to overmix, as this can make the burgers tough.
2. **Form the Patties**: Divide the beef mixture into 8 equal portions. Flatten each portion into a patty, about 1/4 inch thick. Place a few cubes of Irish cheddar cheese in the center of 4 of the patties. Top with the remaining 4 patties and press the edges together to seal, forming a stuffed burger. Make sure the cheese is fully enclosed by the beef.
3. **Cook the Burgers**: Preheat your grill or skillet over medium-high heat. Lightly oil the grill grates or skillet to prevent sticking. Cook the burgers for about 5-7 minutes per side, or until they reach your desired level of doneness and the cheese inside is melted. Avoid pressing down on the burgers while cooking to keep the cheese from leaking out.
4. **Toast the Buns**: During the last few minutes of cooking, place the hamburger buns cut side down on the grill or skillet and toast until golden brown.
5. **Assemble the Burgers**: Place each cooked burger on the bottom half of a toasted bun. Top with lettuce, tomato slices, and pickles. Spread ketchup and mustard on the top bun if desired.
6. **Serve**: Serve the Irish Cheddar Stuffed Burgers immediately while hot and juicy. Enjoy with your favorite sides such as fries or a fresh salad.

These Irish Cheddar Stuffed Burgers combine the rich, tangy flavor of Irish cheddar with the savory goodness of a perfectly cooked burger, creating a deliciously satisfying meal. Enjoy!

Dublin Coddle

Ingredients:

- 1 pound pork sausages (preferably Irish, or use any good-quality sausages)
- 6 slices bacon, chopped
- 4 large potatoes, peeled and sliced into 1/4-inch rounds
- 2 large onions, sliced
- 3 cloves garlic, minced
- 2 cups beef or chicken broth
- 1 cup cold water
- 2 tablespoons fresh parsley, chopped
- 1 teaspoon dried thyme
- 1 bay leaf
- Salt and black pepper to taste

Instructions:

1. **Preheat Oven**: Preheat your oven to 325°F (160°C).
2. **Brown the Sausages and Bacon**: In a large skillet, cook the bacon over medium heat until it starts to crisp, about 5 minutes. Remove the bacon from the skillet and set aside, leaving the fat in the pan. Add the sausages to the skillet and brown them on all sides, about 5-7 minutes. Remove the sausages from the skillet and set aside.
3. **Prepare Vegetables**: In the same skillet, add a little more oil if needed and cook the onions until softened, about 5 minutes. Stir in the minced garlic and cook for an additional minute.
4. **Layer Ingredients**: In a large ovenproof casserole dish or Dutch oven, arrange a layer of potato slices. Season with salt and black pepper. Add a layer of the browned sausages, followed by a layer of the cooked bacon and sautéed onions and garlic. Repeat the layers, finishing with a layer of potatoes on top.
5. **Add Liquids and Seasonings**: Pour the beef or chicken broth and cold water over the layers. Add the dried thyme and bay leaf.
6. **Bake**: Cover the casserole dish or Dutch oven with a lid or aluminum foil. Bake in the preheated oven for 1.5 to 2 hours, or until the potatoes are tender and the flavors are well combined. If you like a crispy top, remove the cover during the last 20 minutes of baking.
7. **Finish and Serve**: Remove the bay leaf and discard. Stir in the fresh parsley. Serve the Dublin Coddle hot, garnished with additional parsley if desired.

Dublin Coddle is a traditional Irish stew, hearty and comforting with layers of sausage, bacon, and potatoes, all simmered together to create a flavorful, satisfying dish. Enjoy this classic comfort food!

Potato and Leek Frittata

Ingredients:

- 2 large potatoes, peeled and diced
- 2 tablespoons olive oil
- 2 leeks, white and light green parts only, sliced thinly
- 6 large eggs
- 1/2 cup milk or heavy cream
- 1 cup shredded cheddar cheese (or other cheese of your choice)
- 1 tablespoon fresh thyme leaves (or 1 teaspoon dried thyme)
- Salt and black pepper to taste
- 1/4 cup fresh parsley, chopped (optional, for garnish)

Instructions:

1. **Preheat Oven**: Preheat your oven to 375°F (190°C).
2. **Cook Potatoes**: In a large ovenproof skillet, heat the olive oil over medium heat. Add the diced potatoes and cook, stirring occasionally, until they are tender and golden brown, about 10-12 minutes. Remove the potatoes from the skillet and set aside.
3. **Sauté Leeks**: In the same skillet, add the sliced leeks and cook until they are softened and lightly caramelized, about 5-7 minutes. Season with salt and black pepper.
4. **Prepare Egg Mixture**: In a large bowl, whisk together the eggs and milk or cream until well combined. Stir in the shredded cheddar cheese, fresh thyme, and additional salt and black pepper to taste.
5. **Combine Ingredients**: Return the cooked potatoes to the skillet with the leeks, mixing them together evenly. Pour the egg mixture over the potatoes and leeks, stirring gently to combine.
6. **Cook Frittata**: Cook the frittata on the stovetop over medium heat for about 5 minutes, until the edges start to set. Transfer the skillet to the preheated oven and bake for 15-20 minutes, or until the frittata is fully set and the top is golden brown.
7. **Cool and Serve**: Let the frittata cool slightly before slicing. Garnish with chopped fresh parsley if desired. Serve warm or at room temperature.

This Potato and Leek Frittata is a versatile and delicious dish, perfect for breakfast, brunch, or a light dinner. The creamy, cheesy interior combined with tender potatoes and leeks makes for a comforting and satisfying meal. Enjoy!

Herb-Crusted Irish Lamb Chops

Ingredients:

- 8 lamb chops (about 1-inch thick)
- 2 tablespoons olive oil
- 1 tablespoon Dijon mustard
- 1 tablespoon fresh rosemary, finely chopped
- 1 tablespoon fresh thyme, finely chopped
- 2 cloves garlic, minced
- 1/2 cup breadcrumbs (preferably from a rustic or whole-grain bread)
- 1/4 cup grated Parmesan cheese
- Salt and black pepper to taste
- Lemon wedges (for serving)

Instructions:

1. **Preheat Oven**: Preheat your oven to 375°F (190°C).
2. **Prepare Lamb Chops**: Pat the lamb chops dry with paper towels and season both sides with salt and black pepper.
3. **Prepare Herb Mixture**: In a small bowl, combine the Dijon mustard, chopped rosemary, thyme, and minced garlic. Stir to combine.
4. **Coat the Lamb**: Brush the Dijon mustard mixture evenly over both sides of the lamb chops.
5. **Prepare the Crust**: In another bowl, mix the breadcrumbs with the grated Parmesan cheese. Press the breadcrumb mixture onto the mustard-coated lamb chops, ensuring an even coating on both sides.
6. **Sear the Lamb Chops**: In an ovenproof skillet, heat the olive oil over medium-high heat. Add the lamb chops and sear for 2-3 minutes per side, until golden brown.
7. **Bake the Lamb Chops**: Transfer the skillet to the preheated oven and bake for 8-12 minutes, depending on your preferred level of doneness. For medium-rare, cook to an internal temperature of 135°F (57°C). For medium, cook to 145°F (63°C).
8. **Rest the Lamb Chops**: Remove the skillet from the oven and let the lamb chops rest for 5 minutes before serving. This helps the juices redistribute throughout the meat.
9. **Serve**: Serve the herb-crusted lamb chops with lemon wedges for squeezing over the top. They pair beautifully with roasted vegetables, mashed potatoes, or a fresh salad.

These Herb-Crusted Irish Lamb Chops offer a delicious combination of savory herbs and tangy mustard, creating a flavorful crust that complements the tender, juicy lamb perfectly. Enjoy this elegant dish for a special occasion or a comforting meal!

Green Veggie Wraps

Ingredients:

- 4 large whole wheat or spinach tortillas
- 1 cup hummus (your favorite flavor, such as classic or lemon)
- 1 cup baby spinach leaves
- 1 cup shredded lettuce
- 1 avocado, sliced
- 1 cucumber, thinly sliced
- 1 cup shredded green cabbage
- 1/2 cup sliced green bell pepper
- 1/4 cup fresh basil leaves (optional, for extra flavor)
- 1 tablespoon olive oil
- Salt and black pepper to taste
- Lemon juice or balsamic vinaigrette (optional, for drizzling)

Instructions:

1. **Prepare the Vegetables**: Wash and slice all the vegetables as needed. If desired, lightly toss the shredded cabbage and green bell pepper in a small bowl with olive oil, salt, and black pepper for added flavor.
2. **Spread the Hummus**: Lay out the tortillas on a flat surface. Spread a generous layer of hummus over each tortilla, leaving about 1 inch from the edges.
3. **Layer the Vegetables**: Evenly distribute the baby spinach, shredded lettuce, avocado slices, cucumber, shredded cabbage, and green bell pepper over the hummus on each tortilla. Add fresh basil leaves if using.
4. **Drizzle (Optional)**: If you like, drizzle a small amount of lemon juice or balsamic vinaigrette over the vegetables for added flavor.
5. **Wrap It Up**: Starting from one end, carefully roll up each tortilla tightly, tucking in the sides as you go to enclose the filling.
6. **Slice and Serve**: Slice each wrap in half diagonally and arrange on a serving platter.

These Green Veggie Wraps are a fresh, nutritious, and flavorful option for lunch or a light dinner. Packed with vibrant vegetables and creamy hummus, they are both satisfying and easy to prepare. Enjoy!

Irish Soda Bread Rolls

Ingredients:

- 4 cups all-purpose flour
- 1/4 cup granulated sugar
- 1 teaspoon baking soda
- 1 teaspoon baking powder
- 1 teaspoon salt
- 1/4 cup cold unsalted butter, cubed
- 1 1/2 cups buttermilk (or 1 1/2 cups milk with 1 1/2 tablespoons lemon juice or white vinegar)
- 1 large egg
- 1 cup raisins or currants (optional)
- 1 tablespoon caraway seeds (optional)

Instructions:

1. **Preheat Oven**: Preheat your oven to 375°F (190°C). Line a baking sheet with parchment paper or lightly grease it.
2. **Mix Dry Ingredients**: In a large bowl, whisk together the flour, sugar, baking soda, baking powder, and salt.
3. **Cut in the Butter**: Add the cold, cubed butter to the dry ingredients. Using a pastry cutter or your fingers, cut the butter into the flour mixture until it resembles coarse crumbs.
4. **Prepare the Wet Ingredients**: In a separate bowl, whisk together the buttermilk and the egg.
5. **Combine Ingredients**: Make a well in the center of the dry ingredients and pour in the wet mixture. Stir gently with a wooden spoon or spatula until just combined. If using raisins or currants and caraway seeds, fold them into the dough at this point.
6. **Form the Rolls**: Turn the dough out onto a lightly floured surface and gently knead it a few times until it holds together. Divide the dough into 12 equal portions and shape each portion into a ball. Place the balls on the prepared baking sheet, spaced about 2 inches apart.
7. **Bake**: Bake in the preheated oven for 20-25 minutes, or until the rolls are golden brown on top and a toothpick inserted into the center comes out clean.
8. **Cool and Serve**: Let the rolls cool on a wire rack for a few minutes before serving. They are best enjoyed warm with a pat of butter.

These Irish Soda Bread Rolls are a delightful and easy-to-make variation of traditional Irish soda bread. With a crisp exterior and a soft, tender interior, they are perfect for breakfast, brunch, or as a side with soups and stews. Enjoy!

Cheddar and Chive Biscuits

Ingredients:

- 2 cups all-purpose flour
- 1 tablespoon baking powder
- 1/2 teaspoon baking soda
- 1/2 teaspoon salt
- 1/2 teaspoon black pepper
- 1/2 cup cold unsalted butter, cubed
- 1 cup shredded sharp cheddar cheese
- 1/4 cup chopped fresh chives
- 3/4 cup buttermilk (or 3/4 cup milk with 3/4 tablespoon lemon juice or white vinegar)

Instructions:

1. **Preheat Oven**: Preheat your oven to 425°F (220°C). Line a baking sheet with parchment paper or lightly grease it.
2. **Mix Dry Ingredients**: In a large bowl, whisk together the flour, baking powder, baking soda, salt, and black pepper.
3. **Cut in the Butter**: Add the cold, cubed butter to the dry ingredients. Using a pastry cutter or your fingers, cut the butter into the flour mixture until it resembles coarse crumbs.
4. **Add Cheese and Chives**: Stir in the shredded cheddar cheese and chopped chives until evenly distributed.
5. **Combine with Buttermilk**: Pour in the buttermilk and gently stir until just combined. Be careful not to overmix; the dough should be slightly lumpy.
6. **Form the Biscuits**: Turn the dough out onto a lightly floured surface and gently pat it into a 1-inch thick rectangle. Use a biscuit cutter or a floured glass to cut out biscuits. Place the biscuits onto the prepared baking sheet, close together but not touching.
7. **Bake**: Bake in the preheated oven for 12-15 minutes, or until the biscuits are golden brown on top.
8. **Cool and Serve**: Let the biscuits cool slightly on a wire rack before serving. They are delicious served warm with butter or as a side to your favorite dishes.

These Cheddar and Chive Biscuits are light, flaky, and packed with savory cheese and fresh herbs, making them a perfect addition to any meal. Enjoy their rich flavor and tender texture!

Sausage and Mash Bites

Ingredients:

- **For the Sausage Filling:**
    - 1 pound (450g) sausage meat or sausages, casings removed
    - 1 small onion, finely chopped
    - 1 clove garlic, minced
    - 1 tablespoon fresh sage, chopped (or 1 teaspoon dried sage)
    - 1 tablespoon vegetable oil
    - Salt and black pepper to taste
- **For the Mashed Potato:**
    - 2 large potatoes, peeled and cubed
    - 1/4 cup milk
    - 2 tablespoons unsalted butter
    - Salt and black pepper to taste
- **For Assembly:**
    - 1/2 cup all-purpose flour
    - 1 large egg, beaten
    - 1 cup breadcrumbs (preferably panko for extra crunch)
    - Vegetable oil, for frying

Instructions:

1. **Cook the Sausage Filling:**
    - In a large skillet, heat the vegetable oil over medium heat. Add the chopped onion and cook until softened and translucent, about 5 minutes.
    - Add the minced garlic and cook for another minute.
    - Add the sausage meat and cook, breaking it up with a spoon, until fully browned and cooked through, about 8-10 minutes. Stir in the chopped sage, and season with salt and black pepper. Remove from heat and let cool slightly.
2. **Prepare the Mashed Potato:**
    - Boil the cubed potatoes in a large pot of salted water until tender, about 15-20 minutes. Drain well.
    - Return the potatoes to the pot and mash with the milk and butter until smooth and creamy. Season with salt and black pepper to taste. Let cool slightly.
3. **Form the Bites:**
    - Preheat your oven to 400°F (200°C).
    - Take a small amount of mashed potato and flatten it into a small patty or disc. Place a small spoonful of sausage filling in the center. Gently fold the mashed potato around the filling to seal it, forming a small ball or bite-sized shape. Repeat with the remaining ingredients.
4. **Bread the Bites:**
    - Dredge each bite in flour, shaking off excess. Dip into the beaten egg, then coat with breadcrumbs, pressing gently to adhere.

5. **Fry or Bake:**
    - **To Fry:** Heat a few inches of vegetable oil in a deep skillet or pan over medium heat. Fry the bites in batches until golden brown and crispy, about 3-4 minutes per side. Drain on paper towels.
    - **To Bake:** Place the breaded bites on a baking sheet lined with parchment paper. Spray lightly with cooking spray or drizzle with a little oil. Bake in the preheated oven for 20-25 minutes, or until golden brown and crisp.
6. **Serve:**
    - Serve the Sausage and Mash Bites warm, with your favorite dipping sauce or as part of a hearty meal.

These Sausage and Mash Bites are a delicious twist on classic comfort food, offering a savory and satisfying treat with a crispy exterior and creamy, flavorful interior. Perfect for parties, snacks, or a fun dinner option!

Spinach and Feta Stuffed Puff Pastry

Ingredients:

- 1 sheet of puff pastry (thawed if frozen)
- 1 tablespoon olive oil
- 1 small onion, finely chopped
- 2 cloves garlic, minced
- 2 cups fresh spinach, chopped
- 1 cup crumbled feta cheese
- 1/4 cup grated Parmesan cheese (optional)
- 1/4 teaspoon ground nutmeg
- Salt and black pepper to taste
- 1 large egg, beaten (for egg wash)
- Sesame seeds or poppy seeds (optional, for garnish)

Instructions:

1. **Preheat Oven**: Preheat your oven to 400°F (200°C). Line a baking sheet with parchment paper.
2. **Prepare the Filling**:
    - Heat the olive oil in a skillet over medium heat. Add the chopped onion and cook until softened and translucent, about 5 minutes.
    - Stir in the minced garlic and cook for another minute.
    - Add the chopped spinach to the skillet and cook until wilted and most of the moisture has evaporated, about 3 minutes. Remove from heat and let cool slightly.
    - In a large bowl, combine the cooked spinach mixture with crumbled feta cheese, Parmesan cheese (if using), ground nutmeg, salt, and black pepper. Mix well.
3. **Prepare the Puff Pastry**:
    - Unfold the puff pastry sheet on a lightly floured surface. Roll it out slightly if needed to smooth out creases.
    - Cut the puff pastry sheet into squares or rectangles, depending on your preference (about 4x4 inches or 5x5 inches works well).
4. **Assemble the Pastries**:
    - Place a spoonful of the spinach and feta filling in the center of each pastry square.
    - Fold the pastry over the filling to create a pocket or fold the edges to form a triangle or rectangle, pressing the edges to seal. You can use a fork to crimp the edges for a decorative touch.
    - Brush the top of each pastry with the beaten egg to give it a golden finish. Sprinkle with sesame seeds or poppy seeds if desired.
5. **Bake**:
    - Arrange the filled pastries on the prepared baking sheet, spacing them about 2 inches apart.

- Bake in the preheated oven for 15-20 minutes, or until the pastries are puffed and golden brown.
6. **Serve**:
    - Allow the pastries to cool slightly before serving. They can be enjoyed warm or at room temperature.

These Spinach and Feta Stuffed Puff Pastries are perfect as a savory appetizer, snack, or light meal. The flaky pastry combined with the creamy, tangy filling creates a deliciously satisfying treat. Enjoy!

Lamb and Mint Meatballs

Ingredients:

- 1 pound (450g) ground lamb
- 1/2 cup fresh mint leaves, finely chopped
- 1/4 cup fresh parsley, finely chopped
- 1/2 small onion, finely chopped
- 2 cloves garlic, minced
- 1/2 cup breadcrumbs (preferably from a crusty bread)
- 1 large egg
- 1 teaspoon ground cumin
- 1/2 teaspoon ground coriander
- 1/2 teaspoon ground cinnamon
- 1/2 teaspoon paprika
- Salt and black pepper to taste
- 2 tablespoons olive oil (for frying or brushing if baking)

Instructions:

1. **Preheat Oven (if baking)**: Preheat your oven to 400°F (200°C) and line a baking sheet with parchment paper.
2. **Mix Meatball Ingredients**:
    - In a large bowl, combine the ground lamb, chopped mint, parsley, onion, garlic, breadcrumbs, and egg.
    - Add the ground cumin, ground coriander, ground cinnamon, paprika, salt, and black pepper.
    - Mix until just combined. Be careful not to overmix, as this can make the meatballs tough.
3. **Form Meatballs**:
    - Shape the mixture into meatballs, about 1 to 1.5 inches in diameter. You should get approximately 20-25 meatballs, depending on size.
4. **Cook the Meatballs**:
    - **To Fry**: Heat olive oil in a large skillet over medium heat. Add the meatballs and cook, turning occasionally, until they are browned on all sides and cooked through, about 10-12 minutes.
    - **To Bake**: Arrange the meatballs on the prepared baking sheet and brush lightly with olive oil. Bake in the preheated oven for 20-25 minutes, or until the meatballs are cooked through and golden brown.
5. **Serve**:
    - Serve the lamb and mint meatballs warm with your choice of sides, such as couscous, rice, or a fresh salad. They are also great with a yogurt sauce or tzatziki for dipping.

These Lamb and Mint Meatballs are aromatic and flavorful, combining the richness of lamb with the fresh, bright notes of mint and herbs. They make for a delicious appetizer, snack, or main course. Enjoy!

Get smarter responses, upload files and images, and more.

Irish Carrot and Parsnip Soup

Ingredients:

- 1 tablespoon olive oil
- 1 large onion, chopped
- 2 cloves garlic, minced
- 4 large carrots, peeled and sliced
- 4 large parsnips, peeled and sliced
- 1 large potato, peeled and diced
- 1 teaspoon ground cumin
- 1/2 teaspoon ground coriander
- 1/2 teaspoon dried thyme
- 4 cups vegetable or chicken broth
- 1 cup water
- Salt and black pepper to taste
- 1/2 cup heavy cream (optional, for creaminess)
- Fresh parsley, chopped (for garnish)

Instructions:

1. **Sauté Vegetables**:
    - In a large pot, heat the olive oil over medium heat. Add the chopped onion and cook until softened and translucent, about 5 minutes.
    - Stir in the minced garlic and cook for another minute until fragrant.
2. **Add Carrots and Parsnips**:
    - Add the sliced carrots, parsnips, and diced potato to the pot. Cook for about 5 minutes, stirring occasionally.
3. **Add Spices and Liquids**:
    - Sprinkle in the ground cumin, ground coriander, and dried thyme. Stir well to coat the vegetables with the spices.
    - Pour in the vegetable or chicken broth and water. Bring the mixture to a boil, then reduce heat and let it simmer until the vegetables are tender, about 20-25 minutes.
4. **Blend the Soup**:
    - Use an immersion blender to puree the soup directly in the pot until smooth. Alternatively, you can carefully transfer the soup in batches to a blender and blend until smooth.
5. **Add Cream (Optional)**:
    - If you prefer a creamier soup, stir in the heavy cream and heat through. Adjust seasoning with salt and black pepper to taste.
6. **Serve**:
    - Ladle the soup into bowls and garnish with chopped fresh parsley. Serve hot with crusty bread or rolls.

This Irish Carrot and Parsnip Soup is a comforting and hearty option, perfect for a cozy meal. The combination of sweet carrots and earthy parsnips creates a rich, flavorful soup that's both satisfying and nutritious. Enjoy!

Corned Beef and Swiss Cheese Panini

Ingredients:

- 4 slices of rye bread
- 4 tablespoons Dijon mustard
- 8 ounces (225g) sliced corned beef
- 4 slices Swiss cheese
- 1/2 cup sauerkraut, drained
- 2 tablespoons butter
- 1 tablespoon mayonnaise (optional, for spreading)

Instructions:

1. **Prepare the Bread**:
   - Spread 1 tablespoon of Dijon mustard on one side of each slice of rye bread. If using mayonnaise, spread it on the other side of each slice.
2. **Assemble the Panini**:
   - On two of the slices of bread, layer the sliced corned beef evenly. Top with Swiss cheese slices and a spoonful of sauerkraut. Place the remaining slices of bread on top, mustard side down, to form sandwiches.
3. **Butter the Bread**:
   - Spread butter on the outside of each slice of bread.
4. **Grill the Panini**:
   - Heat a panini press or a skillet over medium heat. If using a skillet, you can place a heavy pan on top of the sandwiches to press them down.
   - Place the sandwiches in the panini press or skillet. Cook for 3-5 minutes, or until the bread is golden brown and crispy and the cheese is melted. If using a skillet, flip the sandwiches halfway through to ensure even browning.
5. **Serve**:
   - Remove the panini from the press or skillet and let them rest for a minute before cutting. Slice in half and serve hot.

This Corned Beef and Swiss Cheese Panini is a delicious twist on the classic Reuben sandwich, with the tangy Swiss cheese and flavorful corned beef making for a satisfying meal. Perfect for a quick lunch or dinner, especially when paired with a pickle and some coleslaw. Enjoy!

Irish Cheddar and Apple Grilled Cheese

Ingredients:

- 4 slices of rustic sourdough or whole-grain bread
- 2 tablespoons unsalted butter, softened
- 6 ounces (170g) Irish Cheddar cheese, sliced
- 1 medium apple (such as Granny Smith or Honeycrisp), cored and thinly sliced
- 1 tablespoon Dijon mustard (optional)
- 1 tablespoon honey (optional)
- Fresh thyme leaves (optional, for garnish)

Instructions:

1. **Prepare the Bread**:
   - Spread butter evenly on one side of each slice of bread. If using Dijon mustard and honey, spread the mustard on the unbuttered side of two slices of bread and drizzle honey on the other two slices.
2. **Assemble the Sandwich**:
   - Place the cheese slices evenly on the unbuttered side of two slices of bread. Layer the apple slices on top of the cheese. If desired, sprinkle fresh thyme leaves over the apple slices for added flavor.
   - Place the remaining slices of bread on top, buttered side facing out, to form the sandwiches.
3. **Grill the Sandwiches**:
   - Heat a skillet or griddle over medium heat.
   - Place the sandwiches in the skillet and cook for about 3-4 minutes per side, or until the bread is golden brown and the cheese is melted. Press down lightly with a spatula to ensure even grilling.
4. **Serve**:
   - Remove the sandwiches from the skillet and let them cool slightly before slicing in half.
5. **Optional Garnish**:
   - Garnish with additional fresh thyme leaves if desired.

This Irish Cheddar and Apple Grilled Cheese combines the sharp, creamy flavor of Irish Cheddar with the crisp sweetness of fresh apple slices, creating a delightful balance of savory and sweet. Perfect for a comforting lunch or dinner, especially when paired with a bowl of soup or a fresh salad. Enjoy!

Bangers and Mash

Ingredients:

- **For the Bangers:**
    - 8 pork sausages (traditional bangers or your preferred type)
    - 1 tablespoon vegetable oil
- **For the Mash:**
    - 4 large russet or Yukon Gold potatoes, peeled and cubed
    - 1/4 cup milk
    - 2 tablespoons unsalted butter
    - Salt and black pepper to taste
- **For the Onion Gravy:**
    - 2 tablespoons vegetable oil
    - 2 large onions, thinly sliced
    - 2 cloves garlic, minced
    - 2 tablespoons all-purpose flour
    - 1 cup beef or vegetable broth
    - 1 tablespoon Worcestershire sauce
    - 1 teaspoon fresh thyme leaves (or 1/2 teaspoon dried thyme)
    - Salt and black pepper to taste

Instructions:

1. **Cook the Bangers:**
    - Heat the vegetable oil in a large skillet over medium heat.
    - Add the sausages and cook, turning occasionally, until browned and cooked through, about 15-20 minutes. Remove the sausages from the skillet and keep warm.
2. **Prepare the Mash:**
    - Place the cubed potatoes in a large pot of cold, salted water. Bring to a boil over high heat, then reduce to a simmer and cook until the potatoes are tender, about 15-20 minutes.
    - Drain the potatoes and return them to the pot. Add the milk and butter. Mash until smooth and creamy. Season with salt and black pepper to taste. Keep warm.
3. **Make the Onion Gravy:**
    - In the same skillet used for the sausages, heat the vegetable oil over medium heat.
    - Add the sliced onions and cook, stirring frequently, until caramelized and golden brown, about 10-15 minutes.
    - Stir in the minced garlic and cook for an additional minute.
    - Sprinkle the flour over the onions and cook for 1-2 minutes, stirring constantly to form a roux.

- Gradually add the beef or vegetable broth, stirring to avoid lumps. Add the Worcestershire sauce and thyme. Bring to a simmer and cook until the gravy has thickened, about 5-7 minutes. Season with salt and black pepper to taste.
4. **Serve:**
    - Spoon the mashed potatoes onto plates. Top with the sausages and ladle the onion gravy over the top.
    - Garnish with additional fresh thyme if desired.

Bangers and Mash is a classic British dish featuring savory sausages paired with creamy mashed potatoes and a rich onion gravy. It's a hearty and comforting meal that's perfect for any time of year. Enjoy!

Creamy Irish Mushroom Soup

Ingredients:

- 2 tablespoons unsalted butter
- 1 tablespoon olive oil
- 1 large onion, finely chopped
- 3 cloves garlic, minced
- 1 pound (450g) mixed mushrooms (such as button, cremini, and shiitake), sliced
- 1 cup chopped leeks (white and light green parts only), well rinsed
- 4 cups chicken or vegetable broth
- 1 cup heavy cream
- 1 teaspoon fresh thyme leaves (or 1/2 teaspoon dried thyme)
- 1 tablespoon fresh parsley, chopped (for garnish)
- Salt and black pepper to taste
- 1 tablespoon all-purpose flour (optional, for thickening)

Instructions:

1. **Sauté Vegetables**:
    - In a large pot, melt the butter with the olive oil over medium heat. Add the chopped onion and cook until softened and translucent, about 5 minutes.
    - Stir in the minced garlic and cook for another minute until fragrant.
2. **Cook the Mushrooms and Leeks**:
    - Add the sliced mushrooms and chopped leeks to the pot. Cook, stirring occasionally, until the mushrooms are browned and have released their moisture, about 8-10 minutes.
3. **Add Broth and Simmer**:
    - Pour in the chicken or vegetable broth and add the fresh thyme. Bring the mixture to a boil, then reduce heat and let it simmer for 15 minutes.
4. **Blend the Soup**:
    - Use an immersion blender to blend the soup until smooth. Alternatively, you can carefully transfer the soup in batches to a blender and blend until smooth.
5. **Add Cream and Season**:
    - Return the soup to the pot if you used a blender. Stir in the heavy cream and cook over low heat until heated through. If you prefer a thicker soup, you can stir in 1 tablespoon of flour (mixed with a little water to make a slurry) and cook for an additional 5 minutes, stirring constantly.
6. **Season and Garnish**:
    - Season the soup with salt and black pepper to taste. Ladle the soup into bowls and garnish with fresh parsley.
7. **Serve**:
    - Serve the soup hot with crusty bread or a side of your choice.

This **Creamy Irish Mushroom Soup** is rich and flavorful, combining earthy mushrooms with a velvety cream base. It's perfect as a starter for a special meal or as a comforting lunch on a chilly day. Enjoy!

Colcannon Stuffed Mushrooms

Ingredients:

- **For the Colcannon:**
    - 4 large potatoes, peeled and cubed
    - 1/4 cup milk
    - 2 tablespoons unsalted butter
    - 1 cup chopped cabbage (green or savoy)
    - 1/2 cup chopped green onions (scallions)
    - Salt and black pepper to taste
- **For the Stuffed Mushrooms:**
    - 12 large white or cremini mushrooms, stems removed and cleaned
    - 1 tablespoon olive oil
    - 1/2 cup grated Irish Cheddar cheese (or any sharp cheese)
    - 2 cloves garlic, minced
    - 1/4 cup breadcrumbs (optional, for topping)
    - Fresh parsley, chopped (for garnish)

Instructions:

1. **Prepare the Colcannon:**
    - Place the cubed potatoes in a large pot of salted water. Bring to a boil and cook until tender, about 15-20 minutes. Drain and return to the pot.
    - Mash the potatoes with milk and butter until smooth and creamy. Season with salt and black pepper to taste. Set aside.
    - In a skillet, heat a little oil over medium heat. Add the chopped cabbage and cook until wilted and tender, about 5 minutes. Stir in the chopped green onions and cook for an additional 2 minutes. Combine the cabbage mixture with the mashed potatoes. Mix well.
2. **Prepare the Mushrooms:**
    - Preheat your oven to 375°F (190°C). Arrange the mushroom caps on a baking sheet.
    - Brush the mushroom caps lightly with olive oil.
3. **Stuff the Mushrooms:**
    - Spoon a generous amount of the colcannon mixture into each mushroom cap, pressing gently to pack it in.
    - Sprinkle the grated cheese over the top of each stuffed mushroom. If using breadcrumbs, sprinkle them on top of the cheese for added crunch.
4. **Bake:**
    - Bake in the preheated oven for 15-20 minutes, or until the mushrooms are tender and the cheese is melted and bubbly.
5. **Garnish and Serve:**
    - Garnish the stuffed mushrooms with freshly chopped parsley before serving.

These **Colcannon Stuffed Mushrooms** are a delightful twist on traditional colcannon, combining creamy mashed potatoes with savory mushrooms and cheese. They make for a fantastic appetizer or side dish, blending classic Irish flavors with a fun, bite-sized presentation. Enjoy!

Spicy Irish Lamb Sausages

Ingredients:

- **For the Sausage Mix:**
    - 1 pound (450g) ground lamb
    - 1/4 cup fresh parsley, chopped
    - 1 tablespoon fresh thyme leaves (or 1 teaspoon dried thyme)
    - 2 cloves garlic, minced
    - 1 small onion, finely chopped
    - 1 teaspoon ground cumin
    - 1 teaspoon smoked paprika
    - 1/2 teaspoon ground coriander
    - 1/2 teaspoon ground cinnamon
    - 1/2 teaspoon cayenne pepper (adjust to taste for spiciness)
    - 1 teaspoon red pepper flakes (optional, for extra heat)
    - Salt and black pepper to taste
    - 1/4 cup breadcrumbs (optional, for binding)
- **For Cooking:**
    - 1 tablespoon vegetable oil (for frying or grilling)

Instructions:

1. **Prepare the Sausage Mix:**
    - In a large bowl, combine the ground lamb with chopped parsley, thyme, minced garlic, and finely chopped onion.
    - Add the ground cumin, smoked paprika, ground coriander, ground cinnamon, cayenne pepper, and red pepper flakes (if using). Season with salt and black pepper.
    - Mix everything together until well combined. If the mixture feels too loose, add the breadcrumbs to help bind it.
2. **Shape the Sausages:**
    - Divide the sausage mixture into small portions and shape them into sausage links or patties, depending on your preference.
3. **Cook the Sausages:**
    - **To Fry:** Heat the vegetable oil in a skillet over medium heat. Add the sausages and cook, turning occasionally, until they are browned and cooked through, about 10-15 minutes.
    - **To Grill:** Preheat your grill to medium-high heat. Place the sausages on the grill and cook, turning occasionally, until browned and cooked through, about 10-15 minutes.
4. **Serve:**
    - Serve the spicy Irish lamb sausages with your favorite sides such as mashed potatoes, colcannon, or a fresh salad. They also pair well with mustard or a tangy dipping sauce.

These **Spicy Irish Lamb Sausages** bring a robust flavor profile with a touch of heat, making them a delicious and unique addition to any meal. Enjoy them as a flavorful main course or as part of a hearty breakfast spread!

Green Goddess Chicken Salad

Ingredients:

- **For the Chicken Salad:**
    - 2 cups cooked chicken breast, shredded or diced
    - 1/2 cup celery, finely chopped
    - 1/2 cup red grapes, halved (or apple, diced, if preferred)
    - 1/4 cup sliced almonds (optional)
    - 1/4 cup fresh parsley, chopped
- **For the Green Goddess Dressing:**
    - 1/2 cup mayonnaise
    - 1/4 cup plain Greek yogurt (or sour cream)
    - 1/4 cup fresh basil leaves
    - 1/4 cup fresh chives
    - 2 tablespoons fresh lemon juice
    - 1 tablespoon white wine vinegar
    - 1 small garlic clove, minced
    - Salt and black pepper to taste

Instructions:

1. **Prepare the Green Goddess Dressing:**
    - In a food processor or blender, combine the mayonnaise, Greek yogurt, basil, chives, lemon juice, white wine vinegar, and minced garlic.
    - Blend until smooth and creamy. Season with salt and black pepper to taste. Adjust seasoning as needed. Set aside.
2. **Assemble the Chicken Salad:**
    - In a large bowl, combine the cooked chicken, chopped celery, grapes (or apple), sliced almonds (if using), and chopped parsley.
    - Add the Green Goddess Dressing to the chicken mixture and gently toss until everything is well coated.
3. **Serve:**
    - Chill the chicken salad in the refrigerator for at least 30 minutes before serving to allow the flavors to meld.
    - Serve the Green Goddess Chicken Salad on a bed of greens, in a sandwich, or with crackers.

This **Green Goddess Chicken Salad** is a fresh and vibrant dish with a creamy, herb-packed dressing. It's perfect for a light lunch or as a flavorful addition to a picnic or potluck. Enjoy!

Cottage Pie

Ingredients:

- **For the Meat Filling:**
    - 1 tablespoon olive oil
    - 1 large onion, chopped
    - 2 cloves garlic, minced
    - 1 pound (450g) ground beef or lamb
    - 1 carrot, diced
    - 1 celery stalk, diced
    - 1 cup frozen peas
    - 2 tablespoons tomato paste
    - 1 tablespoon Worcestershire sauce
    - 1 cup beef or vegetable broth
    - 1 teaspoon dried thyme
    - 1 teaspoon dried rosemary
    - Salt and black pepper to taste
- **For the Mashed Potato Topping:**
    - 4 large potatoes, peeled and cubed
    - 1/4 cup milk
    - 2 tablespoons unsalted butter
    - Salt and black pepper to taste

Instructions:

1. **Prepare the Mashed Potatoes:**
    - Place the cubed potatoes in a large pot of salted water. Bring to a boil over high heat, then reduce to a simmer and cook until the potatoes are tender, about 15-20 minutes.
    - Drain the potatoes and return them to the pot. Add the milk and butter. Mash until smooth and creamy. Season with salt and black pepper to taste. Set aside.
2. **Cook the Meat Filling:**
    - Heat olive oil in a large skillet over medium heat. Add the chopped onion and cook until softened and translucent, about 5 minutes.
    - Stir in the minced garlic and cook for another minute.
    - Add the ground beef or lamb and cook until browned, breaking it up with a spoon as it cooks.
    - Add the diced carrot and celery, and cook for about 5 minutes until they start to soften.
    - Stir in the tomato paste and cook for 2 minutes.
    - Add the Worcestershire sauce, beef or vegetable broth, dried thyme, and dried rosemary. Bring to a simmer and cook for about 10 minutes, until the sauce has thickened slightly and the vegetables are tender.

- Stir in the frozen peas and cook for another 2 minutes. Season with salt and black pepper to taste.
3. **Assemble and Bake:**
    - Preheat your oven to 400°F (200°C).
    - Spoon the meat filling into a baking dish, spreading it evenly.
    - Carefully spread the mashed potatoes over the top of the meat filling, smoothing it out with a spatula. You can use a fork to create a decorative pattern on top if desired.
    - Place the baking dish in the preheated oven and bake for 20-25 minutes, or until the top is golden brown and the filling is bubbling.
4. **Serve:**
    - Allow the Cottage Pie to cool for a few minutes before serving. Enjoy it hot with a side of green vegetables or a crisp salad.

Cottage Pie is a comforting classic with a savory meat filling and creamy mashed potato topping. It's perfect for a hearty family meal and is sure to please everyone at the table.

Irish Style Tacos

Ingredients:

- **For the Irish Beef Filling:**
    - 1 pound (450g) ground beef
    - 1 tablespoon vegetable oil
    - 1 large onion, finely chopped
    - 2 cloves garlic, minced
    - 1 cup finely chopped cabbage
    - 1 cup shredded carrots
    - 1 tablespoon tomato paste
    - 1 teaspoon ground cumin
    - 1 teaspoon smoked paprika
    - 1/2 teaspoon dried thyme
    - 1 teaspoon Worcestershire sauce
    - 1/2 cup beef broth
    - Salt and black pepper to taste
- **For the Irish Creamy Slaw:**
    - 2 cups shredded cabbage (green or red or a mix)
    - 1/2 cup shredded carrots
    - 1/4 cup mayonnaise
    - 2 tablespoons sour cream or plain Greek yogurt
    - 1 tablespoon apple cider vinegar
    - 1 tablespoon fresh parsley, chopped
    - Salt and black pepper to taste
- **For Serving:**
    - 8 small flour or corn tortillas
    - 1 cup shredded Irish Cheddar cheese (or any sharp cheese)
    - Fresh cilantro, chopped (optional, for garnish)
    - Lime wedges (optional, for serving)

Instructions:

1. **Prepare the Irish Beef Filling:**
    - Heat the vegetable oil in a large skillet over medium heat. Add the chopped onion and cook until softened, about 5 minutes.
    - Stir in the minced garlic and cook for another minute until fragrant.
    - Add the ground beef and cook until browned, breaking it up with a spoon.
    - Stir in the finely chopped cabbage and shredded carrots. Cook for about 5 minutes until the vegetables are tender.
    - Add the tomato paste, ground cumin, smoked paprika, dried thyme, and Worcestershire sauce. Mix well and cook for 2 minutes.
    - Pour in the beef broth and simmer until the mixture thickens slightly, about 5-7 minutes. Season with salt and black pepper to taste.

2. **Prepare the Irish Creamy Slaw:**
    - In a large bowl, combine the shredded cabbage and shredded carrots.
    - In a separate small bowl, whisk together the mayonnaise, sour cream (or Greek yogurt), apple cider vinegar, and fresh parsley. Season with salt and black pepper to taste.
    - Toss the shredded vegetables with the creamy dressing until well coated. Set aside.
3. **Warm the Tortillas:**
    - Heat the tortillas in a dry skillet over medium heat for about 30 seconds on each side until warmed through. Alternatively, you can warm them in the oven wrapped in foil or in the microwave.
4. **Assemble the Tacos:**
    - Spoon the Irish beef filling onto the warmed tortillas.
    - Top with a generous helping of the Irish creamy slaw.
    - Sprinkle with shredded Irish Cheddar cheese.
5. **Serve:**
    - Garnish with fresh cilantro and serve with lime wedges on the side if desired.

Irish Style Tacos offer a unique twist on traditional tacos by incorporating savory Irish flavors like seasoned ground beef and creamy slaw. They're a fun and flavorful way to enjoy a blend of cuisines, perfect for a casual meal or a festive gathering. Enjoy!

Smoked Salmon and Avocado Toast

Ingredients:

- 4 slices of whole-grain or sourdough bread
- 1 ripe avocado
- 1 tablespoon lemon juice (freshly squeezed)
- 1 tablespoon olive oil
- Salt and black pepper to taste
- 4 ounces (115g) smoked salmon, sliced
- 1/4 red onion, thinly sliced
- 1 tablespoon capers (optional)
- Fresh dill or chives, chopped (for garnish)
- Lemon wedges (for serving)

Instructions:

1. **Toast the Bread:**
   - Preheat your toaster or oven to toast the bread slices until they are crispy and golden brown.
2. **Prepare the Avocado Spread:**
   - While the bread is toasting, cut the avocado in half, remove the pit, and scoop the flesh into a bowl.
   - Mash the avocado with a fork until smooth, leaving some chunks if you prefer a bit of texture.
   - Stir in the lemon juice and olive oil. Season with salt and black pepper to taste.
3. **Assemble the Toast:**
   - Spread a generous layer of the avocado mixture over each toasted bread slice.
   - Top with slices of smoked salmon.
4. **Add Garnishes:**
   - Scatter thinly sliced red onion and capers (if using) over the smoked salmon.
   - Garnish with freshly chopped dill or chives.
5. **Serve:**
   - Serve the avocado toast with lemon wedges on the side for an extra touch of freshness.

Smoked Salmon and Avocado Toast combines creamy avocado with the rich, savory flavor of smoked salmon, making for a delightful and nutritious breakfast or brunch. This simple yet elegant dish is perfect for starting your day on a flavorful note or for a quick, satisfying snack. Enjoy!

Irish Sausage Rolls

Ingredients:

- **For the Sausage Filling:**
    - 1 pound (450g) Irish sausages (or your preferred sausages)
    - 1/2 cup fresh breadcrumbs
    - 1 small onion, finely chopped
    - 2 cloves garlic, minced
    - 1 tablespoon fresh parsley, chopped
    - 1 teaspoon dried thyme
    - 1/2 teaspoon dried sage
    - Salt and black pepper to taste
- **For the Pastry:**
    - 1 sheet puff pastry (about 10x10 inches or 25x25 cm), thawed
    - 1 egg, beaten (for egg wash)

Instructions:

1. **Prepare the Sausage Filling:**
    - Remove the sausage meat from the casings and place it in a large bowl. If using pre-cooked sausages, ensure they are fully cooled before removing the casing.
    - Add the fresh breadcrumbs, finely chopped onion, minced garlic, chopped parsley, dried thyme, and dried sage to the sausage meat.
    - Mix everything together until well combined. Season with salt and black pepper to taste. Set aside.
2. **Prepare the Puff Pastry:**
    - Preheat your oven to 400°F (200°C) and line a baking sheet with parchment paper.
    - On a lightly floured surface, roll out the puff pastry sheet to smooth out any creases.
3. **Assemble the Sausage Rolls:**
    - Divide the sausage filling into two equal portions.
    - Place one portion of the sausage filling along one edge of the pastry, creating a long, even strip.
    - Roll the pastry over the sausage filling to form a log or cylinder. Seal the edges by pressing them together gently.
    - Repeat with the second portion of sausage filling.
4. **Cut and Egg Wash:**
    - Cut each pastry log into bite-sized pieces or desired lengths (about 1-2 inches long).
    - Place the sausage rolls on the prepared baking sheet, spacing them apart.
    - Brush the tops of the rolls with the beaten egg to give them a golden, shiny finish.
5. **Bake:**

- Bake in the preheated oven for 20-25 minutes, or until the pastry is golden brown and the sausage filling is cooked through.
6. **Serve:**
    - Allow the sausage rolls to cool slightly before serving. They are delicious warm or at room temperature.

Irish Sausage Rolls are a savory and satisfying treat, perfect for parties, picnics, or a hearty snack. With their flaky pastry and flavorful sausage filling, they offer a comforting and tasty bite that's sure to be a hit with everyone. Enjoy!

Sweet Potato and Kale Soup

Ingredients:

- **For the Soup:**
    - 2 tablespoons olive oil
    - 1 large onion, chopped
    - 2 cloves garlic, minced
    - 2 medium sweet potatoes, peeled and diced
    - 4 cups vegetable broth
    - 1 cup water
    - 1 teaspoon ground cumin
    - 1/2 teaspoon smoked paprika
    - 1/2 teaspoon dried thyme
    - 1/4 teaspoon ground turmeric
    - 1 cup kale, stems removed and leaves chopped
    - Salt and black pepper to taste
    - 1 tablespoon fresh lemon juice (optional, for brightness)
- **For Garnish (optional):**
    - 2 tablespoons plain Greek yogurt or sour cream
    - Fresh parsley or cilantro, chopped
    - Red pepper flakes or a drizzle of olive oil

Instructions:

1. **Sauté the Aromatics:**
    - Heat olive oil in a large pot over medium heat. Add the chopped onion and cook until softened and translucent, about 5 minutes.
    - Stir in the minced garlic and cook for another minute until fragrant.
2. **Cook the Sweet Potatoes:**
    - Add the diced sweet potatoes to the pot and cook for 5 minutes, stirring occasionally.
3. **Add Broth and Seasonings:**
    - Pour in the vegetable broth and water. Stir in the ground cumin, smoked paprika, dried thyme, and ground turmeric.
    - Bring the mixture to a boil, then reduce heat and let it simmer until the sweet potatoes are tender, about 15-20 minutes.
4. **Blend the Soup:**
    - Use an immersion blender to blend the soup until smooth and creamy. Alternatively, you can carefully transfer the soup in batches to a blender and blend until smooth.
5. **Add Kale:**
    - Return the blended soup to the pot (if using a blender). Stir in the chopped kale and cook for an additional 5 minutes, or until the kale is wilted and tender.
6. **Season and Finish:**

- - Season the soup with salt and black pepper to taste. If desired, stir in fresh lemon juice for a bright, tangy flavor.
7. **Serve:**
    - Ladle the soup into bowls. Garnish with a dollop of Greek yogurt or sour cream, fresh parsley or cilantro, and a sprinkle of red pepper flakes or a drizzle of olive oil if desired.

This **Sweet Potato and Kale Soup** is a nutritious and comforting dish with a creamy texture and a touch of earthiness from the kale. It's perfect for a cozy meal on a cool day, offering both flavor and warmth. Enjoy!

Corned Beef Hash

Ingredients:

- 2 tablespoons vegetable oil
- 1 large onion, diced
- 1 red bell pepper, diced
- 2 cloves garlic, minced
- 2 cups cooked corned beef, diced (leftover or store-bought)
- 2 cups cooked potatoes, diced (russet or Yukon Gold, preferably a day or two old)
- 1 teaspoon dried thyme
- 1/2 teaspoon smoked paprika
- Salt and black pepper to taste
- 2 tablespoons fresh parsley, chopped (for garnish)
- 2 large eggs (optional, for serving)
- Hot sauce (optional, for serving)

Instructions:

1. **Cook the Vegetables:**
    - Heat the vegetable oil in a large skillet over medium heat. Add the diced onion and cook until softened and translucent, about 5 minutes.
    - Stir in the diced red bell pepper and cook for another 3 minutes until the peppers are tender.
    - Add the minced garlic and cook for 1 minute until fragrant.
2. **Add the Corned Beef and Potatoes:**
    - Add the diced corned beef to the skillet and cook for 5 minutes, allowing it to crisp up slightly.
    - Stir in the diced potatoes, dried thyme, and smoked paprika. Cook, stirring occasionally, until the potatoes are golden brown and crispy on the edges, about 10-15 minutes.
3. **Season and Finish:**
    - Season the hash with salt and black pepper to taste. Continue cooking for an additional 2-3 minutes, ensuring everything is heated through and well combined.
4. **Optional: Fry the Eggs:**
    - If using eggs, heat a small amount of oil in a separate skillet over medium heat. Crack the eggs into the skillet and cook until the whites are set and the yolks are still runny, or to your desired doneness.
5. **Serve:**
    - Spoon the corned beef hash onto plates or into bowls. Top with a fried egg if desired.
    - Garnish with freshly chopped parsley and serve with hot sauce on the side if you like a bit of extra kick.

Corned Beef Hash is a hearty, flavorful dish that's perfect for breakfast, brunch, or even a satisfying dinner. It combines savory corned beef with crispy potatoes and fresh vegetables, and can be topped with a runny egg for an extra touch of richness. Enjoy!

Green Bean Almondine

Ingredients:

- 1 pound (450g) fresh green beans, trimmed
- 3 tablespoons unsalted butter
- 1/2 cup sliced almonds
- 2 cloves garlic, minced
- 1 tablespoon fresh lemon juice
- 1 teaspoon lemon zest (optional)
- Salt and black pepper to taste
- Fresh parsley, chopped (for garnish)

Instructions:

1. **Blanch the Green Beans:**
   - Bring a large pot of salted water to a boil. Add the green beans and cook for 3-4 minutes, until tender-crisp.
   - Immediately transfer the green beans to a bowl of ice water to stop the cooking process. Let them cool for a few minutes, then drain and pat dry with a paper towel.
2. **Toast the Almonds:**
   - In a large skillet, melt 2 tablespoons of butter over medium heat. Add the sliced almonds and cook, stirring frequently, until they are golden brown and fragrant, about 2-3 minutes. Be careful not to burn them. Remove the almonds from the skillet and set aside.
3. **Sauté the Green Beans:**
   - In the same skillet, melt the remaining 1 tablespoon of butter over medium heat. Add the minced garlic and cook for 1 minute until fragrant.
   - Add the blanched green beans to the skillet and sauté, stirring occasionally, for about 5 minutes until heated through and slightly caramelized.
4. **Combine and Finish:**
   - Return the toasted almonds to the skillet with the green beans. Toss to combine.
   - Stir in the fresh lemon juice and lemon zest (if using). Season with salt and black pepper to taste.
5. **Serve:**
   - Transfer the green bean almondine to a serving dish and garnish with freshly chopped parsley.

Green Bean Almondine is a classic French side dish that's simple yet elegant, featuring tender green beans sautéed with toasted almonds and a touch of lemon. It's a perfect accompaniment to a variety of main courses, adding a delightful crunch and a burst of flavor. Enjoy!

Irish Egg Salad

Ingredients:

- 6 large eggs
- 1/4 cup mayonnaise
- 2 tablespoons plain Greek yogurt (or sour cream)
- 1 tablespoon Dijon mustard
- 1 tablespoon fresh chives, chopped
- 1 tablespoon fresh parsley, chopped
- 1/4 cup finely chopped green onions (scallions)
- 1/4 cup finely chopped celery
- 1/4 teaspoon smoked paprika
- Salt and black pepper to taste
- 1 teaspoon lemon juice (optional, for brightness)
- Lettuce leaves or bread (for serving)

Instructions:

1. **Cook the Eggs:**
    - Place the eggs in a saucepan and cover them with cold water. Bring to a boil over high heat.
    - Once boiling, cover the pan, remove it from heat, and let the eggs sit for 12 minutes.
    - After 12 minutes, transfer the eggs to a bowl of ice water to cool. Once cooled, peel the eggs and chop them into small pieces.
2. **Prepare the Dressing:**
    - In a large bowl, combine the mayonnaise, Greek yogurt (or sour cream), Dijon mustard, chopped chives, chopped parsley, and smoked paprika. Mix well.
    - Season the dressing with salt and black pepper to taste. If using, stir in the lemon juice for added brightness.
3. **Assemble the Salad:**
    - Gently fold the chopped eggs, green onions, and celery into the dressing until well combined.
    - Adjust seasoning with additional salt and pepper if needed.
4. **Serve:**
    - Serve the Irish egg salad on a bed of lettuce leaves, or as a filling for sandwiches or wraps. It also makes a great topping for toast.

Irish Egg Salad offers a creamy, flavorful twist on a classic dish, enhanced with fresh herbs and a touch of tanginess. It's perfect for a light lunch, a picnic, or as a tasty addition to your brunch spread. Enjoy!

Salmon and Dill Quiche

Ingredients:

- **For the Crust:**
    - 1 1/4 cups all-purpose flour
    - 1/2 teaspoon salt
    - 1/2 cup unsalted butter, chilled and cut into small cubes
    - 2-3 tablespoons ice water
- **For the Filling:**
    - 1 tablespoon olive oil
    - 1 small onion, finely chopped
    - 1 cup fresh spinach, chopped
    - 1 cup cooked salmon, flaked (about 6 ounces)
    - 1/2 cup shredded Gruyère or Swiss cheese
    - 1/4 cup fresh dill, chopped
    - 4 large eggs
    - 1 cup heavy cream
    - 1/2 cup milk
    - Salt and black pepper to taste

Instructions:

1. **Prepare the Crust:**
    - In a medium bowl, whisk together the flour and salt. Add the chilled butter and use a pastry cutter or your fingers to blend until the mixture resembles coarse crumbs.
    - Gradually add ice water, 1 tablespoon at a time, until the dough comes together. You may need slightly more or less water.
    - Form the dough into a disk, wrap it in plastic wrap, and refrigerate for at least 30 minutes.
2. **Preheat Oven:**
    - Preheat your oven to 375°F (190°C).
3. **Roll Out the Dough:**
    - On a lightly floured surface, roll out the chilled dough to fit a 9-inch (23 cm) tart pan or pie dish.
    - Gently press the dough into the pan, trimming any excess. Prick the bottom with a fork to prevent bubbling.
4. **Blind Bake the Crust:**
    - Place a sheet of parchment paper over the crust and fill with pie weights or dried beans.
    - Bake in the preheated oven for 15 minutes. Remove the weights and parchment paper, and bake for an additional 5 minutes until the crust is lightly golden. Let it cool slightly.
5. **Prepare the Filling:**

- In a skillet, heat olive oil over medium heat. Add the chopped onion and cook until softened, about 5 minutes.
- Stir in the chopped spinach and cook until wilted. Remove from heat and let it cool slightly.
- In a large bowl, whisk together the eggs, heavy cream, milk, salt, and black pepper.

6. **Assemble the Quiche:**
    - Spread the cooked onion and spinach mixture evenly over the pre-baked crust.
    - Distribute the flaked salmon over the top, followed by the shredded cheese and chopped dill.
    - Pour the egg mixture over the filling, ensuring it's evenly distributed.
7. **Bake:**
    - Bake in the preheated oven for 35-40 minutes, or until the quiche is set and the top is golden brown. A knife inserted into the center should come out clean.
8. **Serve:**
    - Allow the quiche to cool slightly before slicing. Serve warm or at room temperature.

Salmon and Dill Quiche is a flavorful and elegant dish perfect for brunch or a light dinner. The combination of tender salmon, creamy custard, and fresh dill makes for a deliciously satisfying meal. Enjoy!

Savory Irish Pancakes

Ingredients:

- **For the Pancake Batter:**
    - 1 cup all-purpose flour
    - 1 teaspoon baking powder
    - 1/2 teaspoon salt
    - 1 large egg
    - 1 cup milk
    - 2 tablespoons melted butter or vegetable oil
    - 1/2 cup grated Irish Cheddar cheese (or any sharp cheese)
    - 1/4 cup fresh chives or green onions, finely chopped
- **For the Filling (Optional):**
    - 1/2 cup cooked bacon or ham, diced
    - 1/2 cup sautéed mushrooms, sliced
    - 1/2 cup sautéed spinach or kale
- **For Serving:**
    - Sour cream or Greek yogurt
    - Fresh chives, chopped (for garnish)

Instructions:

1. **Prepare the Pancake Batter:**
    - In a large bowl, whisk together the flour, baking powder, and salt.
    - In another bowl, beat the egg and then add the milk and melted butter or oil. Mix well.
    - Pour the wet ingredients into the dry ingredients and stir until just combined. Be careful not to overmix; a few lumps are okay.
    - Fold in the grated cheese and chopped chives or green onions.
2. **Cook the Pancakes:**
    - Heat a non-stick skillet or griddle over medium heat and lightly grease with butter or oil.
    - Pour 1/4 cup of batter onto the skillet for each pancake. Spread slightly into a round shape if needed.
    - Cook until bubbles form on the surface and the edges look set, about 2-3 minutes. Flip and cook for another 1-2 minutes until golden brown and cooked through.
3. **Prepare the Filling (Optional):**
    - If using any fillings, prepare them while the pancakes are cooking. Sauté bacon, ham, mushrooms, or greens in a pan until cooked and tender.
4. **Assemble and Serve:**
    - Once the pancakes are cooked, you can either serve them as is or spread a layer of the optional fillings on one half of the pancake and fold it over.
    - Serve warm with a dollop of sour cream or Greek yogurt on the side.

- Garnish with additional chopped chives if desired.

Savory Irish Pancakes are a delightful twist on the traditional sweet pancake, incorporating sharp Cheddar cheese and fresh herbs for a flavorful breakfast or brunch option. You can customize the fillings to your taste, making them a versatile and satisfying choice for any meal of the day. Enjoy!

Potato, Bacon, and Cheddar Muffins

Ingredients:

- **For the Muffins:**
    - 1 cup all-purpose flour
    - 1 cup whole wheat flour (or use all-purpose flour for a lighter texture)
    - 1 tablespoon baking powder
    - 1/2 teaspoon salt
    - 1/4 teaspoon black pepper
    - 1/2 teaspoon dried thyme (optional)
    - 1 cup grated Cheddar cheese
    - 1 cup cooked bacon, crumbled
    - 1 cup cooked potatoes, peeled and diced (about 1 medium potato)
    - 1/2 cup milk
    - 1/2 cup sour cream or plain Greek yogurt
    - 2 large eggs
    - 1/4 cup melted butter or vegetable oil
- **For Garnish (optional):**
    - Extra shredded Cheddar cheese
    - Fresh chives or parsley, chopped

Instructions:

1. **Preheat Oven:**
    - Preheat your oven to 375°F (190°C). Line a muffin tin with paper liners or lightly grease the cups.
2. **Prepare Dry Ingredients:**
    - In a large bowl, whisk together the all-purpose flour, whole wheat flour, baking powder, salt, black pepper, and dried thyme (if using).
3. **Mix Wet Ingredients:**
    - In another bowl, combine the milk, sour cream or Greek yogurt, eggs, and melted butter or oil. Mix well until smooth.
4. **Combine Ingredients:**
    - Gently fold the grated Cheddar cheese, crumbled bacon, and diced potatoes into the dry ingredients.
    - Pour the wet ingredients into the dry ingredients and stir until just combined. Be careful not to overmix; the batter should be slightly lumpy.
5. **Fill Muffin Tin:**
    - Divide the batter evenly among the muffin cups, filling each about 2/3 full. If desired, sprinkle a little extra shredded Cheddar cheese on top of each muffin for added flavor and a nice crust.
6. **Bake:**
    - Bake in the preheated oven for 20-25 minutes, or until a toothpick inserted into the center of a muffin comes out clean and the tops are golden brown.

7. **Cool and Serve:**
    - Allow the muffins to cool in the tin for 5 minutes, then transfer them to a wire rack to cool completely.
    - Garnish with fresh chopped chives or parsley if desired.

Potato, Bacon, and Cheddar Muffins are savory and satisfying, making them a perfect choice for breakfast, brunch, or as a hearty snack. The combination of crispy bacon, creamy Cheddar, and tender potatoes ensures a delicious, flavorful bite every time. Enjoy!

Irish Chicken Pot Pie

Ingredients:

- **For the Filling:**
    - 2 tablespoons olive oil or butter
    - 1 large onion, diced
    - 2 cloves garlic, minced
    - 2 large carrots, peeled and diced
    - 2 celery stalks, diced
    - 1 cup frozen peas
    - 2 cups cooked chicken, diced (preferably from a rotisserie or leftover roast chicken)
    - 1 cup potatoes, peeled and diced
    - 1/4 cup all-purpose flour
    - 2 cups chicken broth
    - 1/2 cup heavy cream
    - 1 tablespoon fresh thyme leaves
    - 1 tablespoon fresh parsley, chopped
    - Salt and black pepper to taste
- **For the Crust:**
    - 1 sheet of refrigerated or frozen pie dough (or homemade pie crust)
    - 1 egg, beaten (for egg wash)
- **Optional Add-ins:**
    - 1/2 cup shredded Cheddar cheese
    - 1/2 cup cooked bacon, crumbled

Instructions:

1. **Prepare the Filling:**
    - Heat olive oil or butter in a large skillet or saucepan over medium heat. Add the diced onion and cook until softened, about 5 minutes.
    - Stir in the minced garlic and cook for an additional minute.
    - Add the diced carrots and celery, and cook until they start to soften, about 5 minutes.
    - Add the diced potatoes and cook for another 5 minutes.
    - Stir in the flour and cook for 1-2 minutes until it starts to turn golden.
2. **Make the Sauce:**
    - Gradually add the chicken broth while stirring to avoid lumps. Bring the mixture to a boil, then reduce heat and simmer until the potatoes are tender and the sauce has thickened, about 10 minutes.
    - Stir in the heavy cream, fresh thyme, fresh parsley, and frozen peas. Cook for an additional 2-3 minutes until the peas are heated through. Add the cooked chicken and mix well.

- Season the filling with salt and black pepper to taste. Remove from heat and let cool slightly.
3. **Preheat Oven:**
   - Preheat your oven to 375°F (190°C).
4. **Assemble the Pie:**
   - Transfer the chicken filling to a 9-inch (23 cm) pie dish or a similar baking dish.
   - Roll out the pie dough and place it over the filling. Trim any excess dough and crimp the edges to seal.
   - Cut a few slits in the top crust to allow steam to escape.
   - Brush the top with the beaten egg for a golden, shiny finish.
5. **Bake:**
   - Bake in the preheated oven for 30-35 minutes, or until the crust is golden brown and the filling is bubbly.
6. **Cool and Serve:**
   - Allow the pie to cool for a few minutes before serving to let the filling set.

Irish Chicken Pot Pie is a comforting and hearty dish, perfect for a cozy meal. The creamy filling, combined with tender chicken, vegetables, and a golden crust, makes it a satisfying option for dinner. Enjoy the rich flavors and warming goodness of this classic dish!

Broccoli and Cheddar Stuffed Potatoes

Ingredients:

- 4 large russet potatoes
- 1 tablespoon olive oil
- Salt and black pepper to taste
- 1 cup fresh broccoli florets
- 1 cup shredded Cheddar cheese
- 1/4 cup sour cream or plain Greek yogurt
- 2 tablespoons milk
- 2 tablespoons unsalted butter
- 1/4 teaspoon garlic powder (optional)
- 1/4 teaspoon onion powder (optional)
- 1/4 cup chopped fresh chives or green onions (for garnish)

Instructions:

1. **Prepare the Potatoes:**
    - Preheat your oven to 400°F (200°C).
    - Wash and scrub the potatoes. Pat them dry with a paper towel.
    - Pierce each potato several times with a fork. Rub them lightly with olive oil and sprinkle with salt.
    - Place the potatoes directly on the oven rack or a baking sheet and bake for 45-60 minutes, or until they are tender when pierced with a fork.
2. **Prepare the Broccoli:**
    - While the potatoes are baking, steam or blanch the broccoli florets until tender, about 4-5 minutes. Drain and chop into small pieces.
3. **Prepare the Filling:**
    - Once the potatoes are done, remove them from the oven and let them cool slightly.
    - Cut each potato in half lengthwise and scoop out the flesh into a bowl, leaving a small border of potato around the edges.
    - Add the cooked broccoli, shredded Cheddar cheese, sour cream, milk, butter, garlic powder, and onion powder (if using) to the potato flesh. Mash and mix until well combined and creamy. Adjust seasoning with salt and black pepper to taste.
4. **Stuff the Potatoes:**
    - Spoon the broccoli and Cheddar mixture back into the potato skins, mounding it slightly.
    - Place the stuffed potatoes back on the baking sheet.
5. **Bake Again:**
    - Bake in the preheated oven for 15-20 minutes, or until the tops are golden brown and the filling is heated through.
6. **Garnish and Serve:**

- Remove from the oven and let cool slightly. Garnish with chopped fresh chives or green onions before serving.

Broccoli and Cheddar Stuffed Potatoes are a delicious and hearty side dish or main course. The creamy filling, combined with tender broccoli and melted Cheddar, makes these potatoes a flavorful and satisfying choice. Enjoy the comforting blend of flavors and textures in every bite!

Irish Spiced Beef Sandwiches

Ingredients:

- **For the Spiced Beef:**
    - 1 1/2 pounds (680g) beef brisket
    - 2 tablespoons black peppercorns
    - 1 tablespoon coriander seeds
    - 1 tablespoon mustard seeds
    - 1 teaspoon ground allspice
    - 1 teaspoon ground paprika
    - 1 teaspoon ground cloves
    - 1 teaspoon ground cinnamon
    - 4 cloves garlic, minced
    - 2 tablespoons sea salt
    - 2 tablespoons brown sugar
    - 1 cup water
- **For the Sandwiches:**
    - 4-6 slices of crusty Irish soda bread or your choice of sandwich bread
    - 1 tablespoon Dijon mustard
    - 4 tablespoons mayonnaise
    - 1/2 cup thinly sliced pickles
    - 1 cup shredded lettuce or arugula
    - 1 large tomato, thinly sliced
    - Fresh parsley or chives for garnish (optional)

Instructions:

1. **Prepare the Spiced Beef:**
    - Toast the black peppercorns, coriander seeds, and mustard seeds in a dry skillet over medium heat until fragrant, about 2-3 minutes. Let cool, then grind into a coarse powder using a spice grinder or mortar and pestle.
    - In a small bowl, combine the ground spices with allspice, paprika, cloves, cinnamon, minced garlic, sea salt, and brown sugar.
    - Rub the spice mixture all over the beef brisket, covering it evenly. Place the seasoned brisket in a resealable plastic bag or wrap it tightly in plastic wrap. Refrigerate for at least 5 days, turning the meat every day to ensure even curing.
2. **Cook the Spiced Beef:**
    - After curing, preheat your oven to 300°F (150°C).
    - Rinse the spice mixture off the brisket under cold water and pat dry with paper towels.
    - Place the brisket in a roasting pan with 1 cup of water. Cover tightly with aluminum foil.

- Roast in the preheated oven for 3-4 hours, or until the meat is tender and easily shreds with a fork. Remove from the oven and let rest for 10-15 minutes before slicing thinly.
3. **Prepare the Sandwiches:**
    - Toast the slices of Irish soda bread if desired.
    - Spread Dijon mustard on one side of each bread slice and mayonnaise on the other.
    - Layer the sliced spiced beef on the bread, followed by pickles, shredded lettuce or arugula, and tomato slices.
4. **Assemble and Serve:**
    - Close the sandwiches and cut in half if desired. Garnish with fresh parsley or chives if using.
    - Serve immediately or wrap in parchment paper for a portable meal.

Irish Spiced Beef Sandwiches offer a flavorful and robust taste of traditional Irish cuisine. The spiced beef is tender and seasoned to perfection, making it a delicious centerpiece for a hearty sandwich. Perfect for lunch or a satisfying snack, these sandwiches combine the rich flavors of cured beef with fresh and crisp toppings. Enjoy!

Spinach and Irish Cheddar Stuffed Chicken

Ingredients:

- 4 boneless, skinless chicken breasts
- 2 tablespoons olive oil
- 1 cup fresh spinach, chopped
- 1 cup shredded Irish Cheddar cheese
- 1/4 cup cream cheese, softened
- 1 clove garlic, minced
- 1/2 teaspoon dried thyme
- 1/2 teaspoon dried rosemary
- Salt and black pepper to taste
- 1/2 cup grated Parmesan cheese (optional, for topping)
- Toothpicks or kitchen twine (for securing)

Instructions:

1. **Prepare the Stuffing:**
   - In a medium bowl, combine the chopped spinach, shredded Irish Cheddar cheese, softened cream cheese, minced garlic, dried thyme, and dried rosemary. Mix well until the ingredients are evenly combined. Season with salt and black pepper to taste.
2. **Prepare the Chicken Breasts:**
   - Preheat your oven to 375°F (190°C).
   - Using a sharp knife, carefully make a pocket in each chicken breast by cutting horizontally along the thickest side, making sure not to cut all the way through.
3. **Stuff the Chicken:**
   - Spoon the spinach and cheese mixture into each chicken pocket, dividing the filling evenly among the chicken breasts.
   - Secure the openings with toothpicks or kitchen twine to keep the filling inside during cooking.
4. **Cook the Chicken:**
   - Heat the olive oil in a large ovenproof skillet over medium-high heat.
   - Season the outside of each stuffed chicken breast with salt and black pepper.
   - Place the chicken breasts in the skillet and sear for 2-3 minutes on each side, until golden brown.
5. **Bake:**
   - Transfer the skillet to the preheated oven and bake for 20-25 minutes, or until the chicken is cooked through and the internal temperature reaches 165°F (74°C). If using, sprinkle grated Parmesan cheese on top of the chicken during the last 5 minutes of baking for added flavor.
6. **Rest and Serve:**
   - Remove the skillet from the oven and let the chicken breasts rest for 5 minutes before removing the toothpicks or twine.

- - Serve the stuffed chicken with your favorite side dishes, such as roasted vegetables, mashed potatoes, or a simple green salad.

Spinach and Irish Cheddar Stuffed Chicken is a flavorful and elegant dish that combines tender chicken breasts with a creamy and cheesy spinach filling. It's perfect for a special dinner or a comforting meal any night of the week. Enjoy the delicious blend of flavors and textures in each bite!

Green Pea and Mint Soup

Ingredients:

- 2 tablespoons olive oil
- 1 large onion, chopped
- 2 cloves garlic, minced
- 4 cups vegetable or chicken broth
- 4 cups fresh or frozen green peas (about 1 pound or 450g)
- 1 large potato, peeled and diced (for added creaminess)
- 1/2 cup fresh mint leaves, chopped
- 1/2 cup heavy cream or coconut milk (optional, for added creaminess)
- Salt and black pepper to taste
- 1 tablespoon lemon juice (optional, for added brightness)
- Fresh mint leaves for garnish (optional)

Instructions:

1. **Prepare the Base:**
    - In a large pot, heat the olive oil over medium heat. Add the chopped onion and cook until softened and translucent, about 5 minutes.
    - Stir in the minced garlic and cook for another 1 minute until fragrant.
2. **Cook the Vegetables:**
    - Add the diced potato to the pot and cook for 5 minutes, stirring occasionally.
    - Pour in the vegetable or chicken broth and bring to a boil. Reduce heat and simmer for 10 minutes, or until the potatoes are tender.
3. **Add the Peas:**
    - Stir in the green peas and cook for another 5 minutes until the peas are tender.
4. **Blend the Soup:**
    - Using an immersion blender, blend the soup directly in the pot until smooth. Alternatively, you can carefully transfer the soup in batches to a stand blender, blend until smooth, and return it to the pot.
    - If the soup is too thick, add a little more broth or water to reach your desired consistency.
5. **Add Mint and Cream:**
    - Stir in the chopped fresh mint leaves and let the soup simmer for 2-3 minutes to infuse the flavor.
    - If using, add the heavy cream or coconut milk and stir to combine. Season with salt, black pepper, and lemon juice (if using) to taste.
6. **Serve:**
    - Ladle the soup into bowls and garnish with fresh mint leaves if desired.
    - Serve warm, accompanied by crusty bread or a side salad if desired.

Green Pea and Mint Soup is a light, refreshing, and nutritious soup with a vibrant color and a subtle hint of mint. The blend of sweet green peas and aromatic mint makes it a perfect choice for a starter or a light meal. Enjoy the delicate flavors and creamy texture of this simple yet elegant soup!

Irish Breakfast Burritos

Ingredients:

- **For the Filling:**
    - 6 large eggs
    - 1/4 cup milk
    - Salt and black pepper to taste
    - 2 tablespoons butter
    - 4 slices of Irish bacon or regular bacon, cooked and chopped
    - 1 cup cooked breakfast sausage, crumbled (or use Irish bangers if available)
    - 1 cup grated Irish Cheddar cheese
    - 1 cup cooked and diced potatoes (e.g., leftover boiled potatoes or hash browns)
    - 1/2 cup baked beans (optional, for an authentic Irish touch)
    - 1/4 cup fresh chives or parsley, chopped (optional, for garnish)
- **For the Burritos:**
    - 4 large flour tortillas
    - 1/4 cup sour cream (optional, for serving)
    - Salsa or hot sauce (optional, for serving)

Instructions:

1. **Prepare the Filling:**
    - In a medium bowl, whisk together the eggs, milk, salt, and black pepper.
    - Heat butter in a large skillet over medium heat. Pour in the egg mixture and cook, stirring gently, until the eggs are just set but still creamy. Remove from heat and set aside.
2. **Cook the Potatoes:**
    - If not using pre-cooked potatoes, dice and cook the potatoes in the same skillet used for the eggs until golden and crispy. Season with salt and pepper to taste. Remove from the skillet and set aside.
3. **Combine the Ingredients:**
    - In a large bowl, combine the cooked eggs, chopped bacon, crumbled sausage, grated Cheddar cheese, cooked potatoes, and baked beans (if using). Mix well.
4. **Assemble the Burritos:**
    - Warm the flour tortillas in a dry skillet or in the microwave for easier folding.
    - Place a generous portion of the filling mixture in the center of each tortilla.
    - Fold in the sides of the tortilla and roll it up from the bottom, securing the filling inside.
5. **Serve:**
    - Serve the burritos warm, with sour cream and salsa or hot sauce on the side if desired.
    - Garnish with fresh chives or parsley for an added touch of color and flavor.

Irish Breakfast Burritos offer a hearty and satisfying twist on the traditional breakfast burrito, incorporating classic Irish ingredients like bacon, sausage, and Cheddar cheese. Perfect for a filling breakfast or brunch, these burritos are easy to make and packed with flavor. Enjoy the fusion of Irish and Tex-Mex in every bite!

Warm Irish Lentil Salad

Ingredients:

- **For the Salad:**
    - 1 cup green or brown lentils
    - 3 cups water or vegetable broth
    - 1 tablespoon olive oil
    - 1 large onion, finely chopped
    - 2 cloves garlic, minced
    - 1 large carrot, diced
    - 1 cup cherry tomatoes, halved
    - 1/2 cup cooked and crumbled Irish bacon or pancetta (optional)
    - 1 cup fresh spinach or arugula
    - 1/4 cup fresh parsley, chopped
    - 1/4 cup chopped fresh chives (optional)
- **For the Dressing:**
    - 3 tablespoons olive oil
    - 2 tablespoons red wine vinegar or apple cider vinegar
    - 1 tablespoon Dijon mustard
    - 1 teaspoon honey or maple syrup
    - Salt and black pepper to taste

Instructions:

1. **Cook the Lentils:**
    - Rinse the lentils under cold water. In a medium pot, bring 3 cups of water or vegetable broth to a boil.
    - Add the lentils, reduce heat, and simmer for 20-25 minutes, or until tender but still firm. Drain and set aside.
2. **Prepare the Salad Base:**
    - While the lentils are cooking, heat 1 tablespoon of olive oil in a large skillet over medium heat.
    - Add the chopped onion and cook until softened and translucent, about 5 minutes.
    - Stir in the minced garlic and cook for an additional 1 minute.
    - Add the diced carrot and cook for 5-7 minutes, or until the carrot is tender.
    - Add the cherry tomatoes and cook for another 2-3 minutes until they start to soften. If using, stir in the crumbled bacon or pancetta.
3. **Combine the Salad:**
    - In a large bowl, combine the cooked lentils with the sautéed vegetables and bacon.
    - Stir in the fresh spinach or arugula and let it wilt slightly from the warmth of the lentils and vegetables.
    - Add the chopped parsley and chives (if using).
4. **Prepare the Dressing:**

- In a small bowl or jar, whisk together the olive oil, red wine vinegar, Dijon mustard, honey, salt, and black pepper until well combined.
5. **Toss and Serve:**
    - Drizzle the dressing over the warm lentil salad and toss to combine thoroughly.
    - Serve warm or at room temperature.

Warm Irish Lentil Salad is a hearty, nutritious dish that combines the earthy flavors of lentils with fresh vegetables and a tangy dressing. It's perfect as a main course or a side dish, offering a comforting and satisfying meal that highlights wholesome ingredients. Enjoy the balance of flavors and textures in this wholesome salad!

Mushroom and Barley Soup

Ingredients:

- **For the Soup:**
    - 2 tablespoons olive oil
    - 1 large onion, diced
    - 2 cloves garlic, minced
    - 3 cups mushrooms, sliced (such as cremini, button, or a mix)
    - 2 medium carrots, diced
    - 2 celery stalks, diced
    - 1 cup pearl barley
    - 6 cups vegetable or chicken broth
    - 1 cup water (or more broth if needed)
    - 1 teaspoon dried thyme
    - 1 teaspoon dried rosemary
    - 1 bay leaf
    - Salt and black pepper to taste
    - 1 tablespoon soy sauce or tamari (optional, for added umami)
    - 1/4 cup fresh parsley, chopped (for garnish)
    - 1 tablespoon lemon juice (optional, for brightness)

Instructions:

1. **Prepare the Base:**
    - Heat the olive oil in a large pot over medium heat. Add the diced onion and cook until softened and translucent, about 5 minutes.
    - Stir in the minced garlic and cook for another minute until fragrant.
2. **Cook the Vegetables:**
    - Add the sliced mushrooms, diced carrots, and diced celery to the pot. Cook, stirring occasionally, until the mushrooms release their moisture and start to brown, about 8 minutes.
3. **Add Barley and Broth:**
    - Stir in the pearl barley and cook for 2 minutes to lightly toast it.
    - Add the vegetable or chicken broth, water, dried thyme, dried rosemary, and bay leaf. Bring the mixture to a boil.
4. **Simmer:**
    - Reduce the heat to low and let the soup simmer, uncovered, for 30-35 minutes, or until the barley is tender and the vegetables are cooked through. Add more water or broth if the soup becomes too thick.
5. **Season and Finish:**
    - Season the soup with salt, black pepper, and soy sauce or tamari (if using) to taste.
    - Stir in the chopped fresh parsley and lemon juice (if using) for added brightness.
6. **Serve:**

- Ladle the soup into bowls and garnish with additional parsley if desired.
- Serve warm with crusty bread or a side salad.

Mushroom and Barley Soup is a hearty, comforting dish that combines the rich umami flavor of mushrooms with the nutty texture of barley. This wholesome soup is perfect for a cozy meal, offering both nourishment and depth of flavor. Enjoy the satisfying and earthy flavors of this classic soup!

Cabbage and Apple Slaw

Ingredients:

- **For the Slaw:**
    - 4 cups green cabbage, shredded
    - 1 cup red cabbage, shredded (optional, for color)
    - 1 large apple, cored and julienned (a crisp variety like Granny Smith or Honeycrisp works well)
    - 1 medium carrot, peeled and shredded
    - 1/4 cup red onion, finely chopped
    - 1/4 cup fresh parsley, chopped (optional, for garnish)
- **For the Dressing:**
    - 1/4 cup apple cider vinegar
    - 2 tablespoons honey or maple syrup
    - 2 tablespoons Dijon mustard
    - 1/4 cup mayonnaise (or Greek yogurt for a lighter option)
    - 2 tablespoons olive oil
    - Salt and black pepper to taste

Instructions:

1. **Prepare the Vegetables and Apple:**
    - In a large bowl, combine the shredded green cabbage, red cabbage (if using), julienned apple, shredded carrot, and finely chopped red onion.
2. **Make the Dressing:**
    - In a small bowl or jar, whisk together the apple cider vinegar, honey or maple syrup, Dijon mustard, mayonnaise (or Greek yogurt), and olive oil until well combined and smooth.
    - Season with salt and black pepper to taste.
3. **Toss the Slaw:**
    - Pour the dressing over the cabbage and apple mixture. Toss well to ensure everything is evenly coated with the dressing.
4. **Chill and Serve:**
    - For best results, cover the slaw and refrigerate for at least 30 minutes before serving to allow the flavors to meld and the cabbage to slightly soften.
    - Garnish with chopped fresh parsley if desired before serving.

Cabbage and Apple Slaw is a refreshing and crunchy side dish that balances the tanginess of apple cider vinegar with the sweetness of apples and honey. The combination of crisp cabbage, juicy apple, and a creamy dressing makes this slaw a perfect accompaniment to a variety of dishes, from grilled meats to sandwiches. Enjoy the vibrant flavors and textures of this easy-to-make slaw!

Irish Smoked Fish Chowder

Ingredients:

- **For the Chowder:**
    - 2 tablespoons butter
    - 1 large onion, diced
    - 2 cloves garlic, minced
    - 2 stalks celery, diced
    - 1 large carrot, peeled and diced
    - 4 cups potatoes, peeled and diced (about 1/2-inch cubes)
    - 4 cups fish stock or chicken broth
    - 1 cup whole milk or heavy cream
    - 1 cup smoked fish, such as smoked haddock or salmon, flaked and bones removed
    - 1 cup corn kernels (fresh, frozen, or canned)
    - 1 teaspoon dried thyme
    - 1 bay leaf
    - Salt and black pepper to taste
    - 2 tablespoons fresh parsley, chopped (for garnish)
    - 1 tablespoon lemon juice (optional, for brightness)

Instructions:

1. **Prepare the Base:**
    - In a large pot or Dutch oven, melt the butter over medium heat. Add the diced onion and cook until softened and translucent, about 5 minutes.
    - Stir in the minced garlic and cook for an additional 1 minute until fragrant.
2. **Cook the Vegetables:**
    - Add the diced celery and carrot to the pot and cook for 5 minutes, stirring occasionally.
    - Add the diced potatoes and cook for another 5 minutes.
3. **Add Broth and Simmer:**
    - Pour in the fish stock or chicken broth and add the dried thyme and bay leaf. Bring the mixture to a boil.
    - Reduce the heat and simmer for 15-20 minutes, or until the potatoes are tender.
4. **Incorporate the Fish and Corn:**
    - Stir in the flaked smoked fish and corn kernels. Cook for another 5 minutes until the fish is heated through and the corn is tender.
    - Stir in the whole milk or heavy cream and cook for an additional 2-3 minutes, just to heat the chowder through. Do not allow it to boil after adding the cream to prevent curdling.
5. **Season and Finish:**
    - Season the chowder with salt and black pepper to taste.
    - Stir in the fresh parsley and lemon juice if using, for added brightness.

6. **Serve:**
    - Ladle the chowder into bowls and garnish with additional fresh parsley if desired.
    - Serve hot with crusty bread or crackers on the side.

Irish Smoked Fish Chowder is a rich and comforting dish that brings together the smoky flavors of fish with the creamy texture of a classic chowder. Perfect for a hearty meal, this chowder showcases the best of Irish seafood with its warming and satisfying qualities. Enjoy the robust flavors and creamy goodness of this traditional Irish favorite!

Green Pesto Pasta with Irish Cheddar

Ingredients:

- **For the Pesto:**
    - 2 cups fresh basil leaves
    - 1/2 cup fresh parsley leaves
    - 1/2 cup pine nuts or walnuts
    - 1/2 cup grated Irish Cheddar cheese
    - 1/2 cup extra virgin olive oil
    - 2 cloves garlic
    - 1 tablespoon lemon juice
    - Salt and black pepper to taste
- **For the Pasta:**
    - 12 ounces (340g) pasta (such as penne, fusilli, or spaghetti)
    - 1 cup cherry tomatoes, halved (optional)
    - 1 cup fresh spinach or arugula (optional)
    - Additional grated Irish Cheddar cheese for serving

Instructions:

1. **Prepare the Pesto:**
    - In a food processor or blender, combine the basil leaves, parsley leaves, pine nuts (or walnuts), grated Irish Cheddar cheese, garlic, and lemon juice.
    - Pulse until the mixture is finely chopped.
    - With the processor running, slowly drizzle in the olive oil until the pesto is smooth and well combined. Scrape down the sides as needed.
    - Season with salt and black pepper to taste. Set aside.
2. **Cook the Pasta:**
    - Bring a large pot of salted water to a boil. Cook the pasta according to the package instructions until al dente.
    - Reserve 1/2 cup of pasta cooking water, then drain the pasta.
3. **Combine Pasta and Pesto:**
    - Return the drained pasta to the pot or a large bowl.
    - Add the green pesto and toss to coat the pasta evenly. If the pesto is too thick, gradually add some of the reserved pasta water until the sauce reaches your desired consistency.
    - If using, gently fold in the halved cherry tomatoes and fresh spinach or arugula.
4. **Serve:**
    - Transfer the pesto pasta to serving plates or bowls.
    - Garnish with additional grated Irish Cheddar cheese.
    - Serve immediately.

Green Pesto Pasta with Irish Cheddar combines the vibrant flavors of fresh basil and parsley pesto with the rich, tangy taste of Irish Cheddar cheese. This dish is a delightful fusion of Italian and Irish ingredients, offering a creamy and flavorful pasta experience. Enjoy the simplicity and elegance of this easy-to-make recipe!

www.ingramcontent.com/pod-product-compliance
Lightning Source LLC
LaVergne TN
LVHW062048070526
838201LV00080B/2258